PORTRAIT OF
ELLEN TERRY

LETTIE HARDY

RUTH MEADOWS

JULIET

QUEEN HENRIETTA MARIA

OPHELIA

BEATRICE

PORTIA

JANETTE

Horace Morehen
1883

DAVID F.
CHESHIRE

Portrait of
Ellen Terry

AMBER LANE PRESS

Frontispiece: Horace Morchen's 1883 drawing of Ellen in some of the roles she played in her first five seasons at the Lyceum. *Clockwise from the top:* Ruth Meadows (*Eugene Aram*); Juliet (*Romeo and Juliet*); Ophelia (*Hamlet*); Jeanette (*The Lyons Mail*); Portia (*The Merchant of Venice*); Beatrice (*Much Ado About Nothing*); Queen Henrietta Maria (*Charles I*); Letitia Hardy (*The Belle's Stratagem*). *Centre:* Portia.

PICTURE CREDITS

By courtesy of the Trustees of the British Library: 60 bottom left, bottom right, 66, 68, 72 bottom, 76, 78 top, bottom, 80. *By courtesy of the Trustees of the British Museum:* 48. *David F. Cheshire:* 6, 8, 9, 11, 14, 15, 16 left, right, 17 bottom, 29, 34, 36, 46, 49, 56, 62 left, 71, 74, 75, 77, 79 top, bottom, 83 top right, bottom, 82, 84 left, 85, 86, 89 top right, bottom, 95 left, 102, 109, 112 left, right, 114, 115, 117. *Ellen Cheshire:* 31 top left. *Edward Craig:* 2, 10 right, 13, 19, 33, 43, 47 right, 50, 52, 58, 67 top, bottom left, bottom right, 69, 72 top right, 73, 83 top left, 95 right, 97 top, bottom, 98, 100 top, 101, 113 right, 118. *The Fine Art Society, London:* 47 left. *Garrick Club/E. T. Archive:* 10 left, 55, 64, 93. *Gernsheim Collection:* 31 top right. *Hon. Mrs. B. A. F. Hervey-Bathurst, Eastnor Castle, Ledbury, Herefordshire:* 23. *E. A. Horner Library:* 104. *The Raymond Mander and Joe Mitchenson Theatre Collection:* 42, 62 right, 63, 81, 100 bottom. *Motley Books:* 51. *By courtesy of the Trustees of the National Portrait Gallery:* 27, 70. *The National Trust:* 21. *Royal Academy of Arts:* 59. *Sotheby's:* 26, 28, 113 left. *By courtesy of the Trustees of the Tate Gallery:* 72 top left. *University of Bristol Theatre Collection:* front cover, 24, 44, 90, 107. *By courtesy of the Board of Trustees of the Victoria and Albert Museum:* 17 top, 20 left, right, 31 bottom, 32, 35, 38, 39 left, centre, right, 60 top, 84 right, 89 top left, 108.

Every effort has been made by the Publishers to observe the legal requirements of suppliers of photographic materials.

Published in 1989 by Amber Lane Press Ltd,
Church Street, Charlbury, Oxford OX7 3PR

Typeset in Perpetua and printed and bound in Great Britain
by Netherwood Dalton & Co Ltd, Bradley Mills, Huddersfield, W Yorks

Copyright © David F. Cheshire, 1989

ISBN: 0 906399 93 9

Contents

Acknowledgements

The following individuals must be thanked for their help given in various ways on various specific points and general ideas at various times over the lengthy period of research for this book: Geoffrey Ashton; Shirley Bury; Dorothea Clover; H. E. R. Craig; Madeleine Ginsberg; Tony Latham; Valerie Mendes; Terence Pepper; Christopher Robinson and Mrs. Molly Thomas. The Librarians and Archivists at the British Library; the General Register Office; Glasgow District Libraries; Liverpool Record Office; the National Film Archive; Portsmouth Public Library; the *Punch* Library; the War Office and Wolverhampton Public Library have been as helpful as Librarians and Archivists always are.

Above all I must thank Edward Craig (Ellen Terry's grandson) for his extraordinarily generous support, advice and, especially, the loan of so many photographs without which the visual impact of the book would have been much the poorer.

Finally this book would not have been possible if my wife and children — Joy, Ellen and Henry — had not allowed me to disappear into Lyceum-land quite so often.

David F. Cheshire
London, 1989

Ellen's son, Edward Gordon Craig, created this woodcut, which was used on the cover of the programme for the Ellen Terry Memorial Matinée at the Palace Theatre on 23rd April, 1929. Scattered among the flowers are the initials of some of the more important people in her life.

Introduction

ELLEN TERRY was the leading British actress of the last quarter of the nineteenth century and Henry Irving was the leading British actor. When they joined forces at the Lyceum Theatre in London in 1878 Irving was already a figure of some eminence, with over 600 roles in his repertoire. He had a magnetic and somewhat sardonic personality, both onstage and off, and had cultivated an image as an intelligent and respected spokesman for the theatre. He was also a spectacular producer; his first nights in particular were immensely successful, well-publicised affairs upon which he lavished considerable time, effort and expense.

The reputation of each Lyceum season and tour really depended, as Winston Churchill observed, upon "the happy conjunction of [Ellen Terry's] gay and charming genius with the mysterious and sinister grace of Henry Irving."

Ellen Terry's image was one of an attractive but erratic charmer. Like her obvious successors, the Hollywood love-goddesses, she built up an affectionate following through sheer strength of personality. She did not have the grand Comédie Française manner which to the French (and Henry James) signified a real actress. For them she was too 'natural'. But Sarah Bernhardt summed it up: "She is not a great actress, but she is more a woman than all the women in the world."

Her son Edward Gordon Craig maintained that, "She played but one part — herself; and when not herself, she couldn't play it." The same was also said of Irving and it is true of many actors; they are all playing roles on both sides of the curtain.

George Bernard Shaw discussed Ellen's stage persona in an essay on her sister, Kate Terry:

> Ellen Terry, whose keenness of intelligence is beyond
> all dissimulating, has often succeeded in making eminent
> critics believe that her stagecraft and nervous athleticism
> are mere efflorescences of her personal charm.

A LESSON IN DEPORTMENT

A caricature of Ellen learning to dance in Sardou's *Madame Sans-Gêne*, 1897. Horace Morchen has exaggerated the serpentine swirl of her movement but the picture does give an excellent idea of the effect produced by wearing extra-long dresses on stage. Norman Forbes is her dancing master.

Craig observed a distinct personality split:

> Nelly and Ellen Terry were and are two. The elder of the two was the great and famous actress — the important figure known to everyone, admired by all and by me: the young one was the little girl Nelly — known to hardly anyone — my mother — and adored by me.

He was right — Ellen could be childlike — but he was wrong to assume that only he saw this side of her. She was forever playing pranks. Alfred Sutro tells the story of an incident in *Ravenswood* when Ellen tripped and started giggling. Irving had to struggle through the rest of the scene on his own but it was she who got the extra round of applause at the end.

Sir Frank Benson recalled a similar offstage event:

> I have seen her, in one of her irresponsible moods, catch hold of a bit of scenery that was being hoisted to the flies, hanging on with her lithe strong arms and graceful figure until she was some forty feet above the stage. The terror-stricken carpenters hastened to lower their precious burden so soon as they perceived that they were hauling heavenward one of the mainstays of the Lyceum. The only answer she vouchsafed to the perplexed managers and anxious friends was an impromptu Irish jig, to show how much better she felt for her aerial flight.

How did she achieve her effects on stage? By well-rehearsed 'natural' delivery of speech, cleverly designed costumes and almost constant movement. If it is remembered that when she made a recording in 1911, she was sixty-four, forced to stand still, lacked the usual Lyceum background music, and had not adapted her theatre-filling style for the microphone, her delivery still sounds as natural as that of most modern actresses.

Right: This striking portrait of his mother was Edward Gordon Craig's third published woodcut. The picture was given away free with the December 1898 issue of *The Dome.*

Left: Ellen in 1883 at the peak of her fame and, according to Marguerite Steen, on the verge of a nervous breakdown. *Right:* Hayman Seleg Mendelssohn was the photographer who pioneered the use of artificial illumination at close quarters. His 1888 portrait of Ellen is, therefore, a perfect example of how the use of flattering lighting and the 'correct' camera angle can transform a personable face into something more conventionally glamorous. Ellen is wearing many rings, as was her custom, including an intaglio seal ring, and the double snake ring (a serpent biting its tail as a symbol of eternity) that features in Julia Margaret Cameron's photograph Sadness' of 1864.

Every new generation of English-speaking actors is regarded as more natural than the last, of course. In the 1950's Marlon Brando, for example, was greeted as the last word in 'natural' speaking and behaviour; thirty years on his staginess is obvious. But Ellen's gramophone records still catch vestiges of that younger, sexier voice so well described by Henry James: "[It] has a sort of monotonous husky thickness which is extremely touching, though it gravely interferes with the modulation of her speeches."

The care that Ellen took with her stage costumes ensured that they were easy to wear and completely suited to the visual effect required. W. Graham Robertson remembered in detail one costume that she wore in *Becket*:

> She looked her loveliest in the rich gown of her first
> entrance, a wonderful, Rossettian effect of dim gold and
> glowing colour veiled in black, her masses of bright hair

in a net of gold and golden hearts embroidered on her robe . . . . The foundation was an old pink gown, worn with stage service and reprieved for the occasion from the rag-bag. The mysterious veiling was the coarsest and cheapest black net, the glory of her hair through golden meshes was a bag of gold tinsel stuffed with crumpled paper, and the embroidered gold hearts were cut out of gold paper and gummed on. The whole costume would have been dear at ten shillings and was one of the finest stage dresses that I have ever seen.

Many of Ellen's costumes were designed by Mrs Alice Comyns Carr and Ellen invariably bombarded her with letters throughout the design and manufacturing process. On 4th March, 1891, for example, she wrote to the seamstress about a yellow dress she was due to wear as Queen Henrietta in *Charles I*:

> Remind Mrs Carr about the length — it must be too long behind for grace must not be left out for all the archiology [*sic*] in the world — the breadth of that dress is great, and so it must be kept long — especially as I hold it over my arm a good deal.

The extra length also produced two other telling effects. Firstly, it emphasised the speed with which Ellen moved around the stage. Some commentators maintained that both she and Irving seemed to dance

Mary Miles' sketches — and their captions: 'Yes, I know that I am charming.' and 'Playfully tossed it out of the window.' — neatly epitomise the more expansive side of Ellen's personality that so dismayed Sir Henry Irving's son.

rather than walk through their scenes. She retained this ability to move gracefully and swiftly, and Edith Evans recalled: ''Whenever she moved, she was lovely to look at, and whenever she stopped she was always pictorial; it was so natural to her, she didn't pose to be pictorial.''

Secondly, the long dresses were used to accentuate her height. Ellen was tall for an actress at about 5 ft 6 ins (both Marie Lloyd and Sarah Bernhardt were barely 5 ft) and her costumes were designed to draw attention away from other features that were considered less than perfect. Charles Reade listed these in his 1875 notebook:

> Ellen Terry is an enigma. Her eyes are pale, her nose rather long, her mouth nothing particular. Complexion a delicate brick-dust, her hair rather like tow. Yet somehow she is *beautiful*. Her expression kills any pretty face you see beside her. Her figure is lean and bony, her hand masculine in size and form yet she is a pattern of fawn-like grace . . .

Offstage Ellen was undoubtedly unconventional. She rarely wore make-up and as she eschewed corsets and tight-fitting clothes almost completely after 1870 her figure was always unfashionably mature. Because she seemed close to the Venus de Milo ideal she was much admired by painters and poets. Unfortunately, with the exception of G. F. Watts (her first husband) and Oscar Wilde, her admirers rarely produced anything worthwhile, either on canvas or in print.

Ellen always preferred the 'artistic' or 'aesthetic' style to high fashion. In her autobiography she described her years in the country with her lover E. W. Godwin: ''I went to church in blue-and-white cotton, with my servant in silk. 'I don't half like it,' she said. 'They'll take you for the cook and me for the lady!' ''

The 'bohemian' look did have an influence on many rebellious young women who admired Ellen's high spirits. Lady Asquith met her at a party on 25th April, 1916, and remarked:

> She is too delicious and fascinating — a child with such marvellous bubbling-over vitality. It was like having an electric battery in the room and one felt ashamed of being the slug one is.

A quarter of a century earlier Ellen had had just the same effect at a party at which Thomas Hardy was a guest. He was captivated:

> Presently Ellen Terry arrived — diaphanous — a sort of balsam, or sea-anemone without shadow . . . like a machine in which, if you press a spring, all the works fly open . . .

Photographer R. Thrupp of Birmingham captured Ellen in an informal mood when she was on tour in 1881. Her short hair and casual woollen sweater set the trend for many young women who followed her lead in dressing to please themselves rather than their mothers.

1. The Early Years

Left: Portrait by a Miss Bond of Southsea, possibly taken when Ellen was visiting her grandparents in 1856.

BEN TERRY, Ellen's father, was the son of an Irish publican, and Sarah Ballard, her mother, was the daughter of a Scottish builder. Both families were settled in Portsmouth and attended the local Wesleyan Meeting House. In 1837 Benjamin joined the orchestra at the local Theatre Royal and a year later he and Sarah were married — against her parents' wishes and without his parents' knowledge. Both claimed to be twenty-one for the occasion: they were, in fact, nineteen and twenty respectively.

The young couple set forth immediately as strolling players. By the time [Alice] Ellen Terry was born, in Coventry on 27th February, 1847, her parents had established themselves in the provinces. Ellen had an older brother and sister — Ben (born in 1839) and Kate (born in 1844). Two other children had died in infancy.

Both daughters were coached by their father and in 1852 Kate secured a contract with Charles Kean at the Princess's Theatre in London. Sarah set off with Kate and young Benjamin while Ellen stayed with her father in Liverpool where he had a season's engagement to complete. Ellen recalled:

> He never ceased teaching me to be useful, alert and quick . . . . he always corrected me if I pronounced any word in a slipshod fashion. He himself was a beautiful elocutionist, and if I now speak my language well it is in no small degree due to my early training.

Ellen's father joined Kean's company himself in 1853 and the family took an apartment in Gower Street. Ellen too was soon seen at the Princess's Theatre. She is reputed to have appeared as the Duke of York (one of the little princes in the Tower) in *Richard III* in 1854.

In 1856 Ellen auditioned successfully for the part of Mamillius in *The Winter's Tale* at the Princess's Theatre. This has never been one of Shakespeare's more popular plays but the production ran for 102 consecutive nights. Ellen acquitted herself well on the first night, which was attended by Queen Victoria and Prince Albert. *The Times* (1st May, 1856) commented on her ''vivacious precocity that proves

The theatrical lodgings (with eating-house below) at 5 Market Street, Coventry, where Ellen was born. The building was blitzed in 1942.

her a worthy relative of her sister.'' But her performance was not without incident, as Ellen herself recalled:

> When Mr Kean as Leontes told me to 'go play', I obeyed his instructions with such vigour that I tripped over the handle [of the cart] and came down on my back! A titter ran through the house, and I felt that my career as an actress was ruined.

Lewis Carroll was not at the first night but he was there on 16th June, when he ''. . . especially admired the acting of the little Mamillius, Ellen Terry, a beautiful creature who played with remarkable ease and spirit.''

Ellen's next part at the Princess's was in *A Midsummer Night's Dream*. The reviewer in *The Illustrated Times* proclaimed that her stage personality was already established:

> A little girl . . . played Puck better than I have ever yet seen the trying part filled; there was a clearness of voice, a gracefulness of pose, and a hearty appreciation of the mischief she was causing.

Left: Ellen as Mamillius with Charles Kean as Leontes in his production of *The Winter's Tale*, which opened at the Princess's Theatre on 28th April, 1856. She is pulling the little cart over which she tripped on the first night. Photograph by Martin Laroche. *Right:* In 1906 Ellen played Hermione with Philip Tonge as the young Mamillius.

A watercolour by Thomas Grieve of the typically lavish set
by Frederick Lloyds for the palace of Theseus in Charles
Kean's production of *A Midsummer Night's Dream*, 1856.
Ellen as Puck is represented by the small figure in the front
row.

Right: Ellen as Puck, photographed by Adolphe Beau.

Ellen played Puck for 250 consecutive nights and later admitted she became ''a bit of a romp . . . vain and rather cocky'', but the management doubled her salary to thirty shillings a week after she had carried on acting during one performance when she caught her foot painfully in a trap-door.

With three members of the family working regularly the Terrys were able to move to a better house, at 92 Stanhope Street in Camden Town. Ben and Sarah spent the rest of their lives there. Ellen and Kate continued at the Princess's, walking on in most productions and playing featured roles whenever the opportunity occurred.

In 1857 Ben hired the Theatre Royal in Ryde on the Isle of Wight for the summer and presented his two daughters as children playing adult roles in *A Drawing-Room Entertainment*. Ellen and Kate were now popular enough to attract audiences in their own right and the season was a huge success. In 1859 they appeared at the Olympic Theatre in Tom Taylor's *Nine Points of the Law*. The engagement was to prove crucial for both sisters as Tom and Laura Taylor kept open house at their home near Clapham Common, where Ellen and Kate were frequent visitors. They were soon absorbed into a circle of artists and writers and the London *beau monde*.

Ben continued to present *A Drawing-Room Entertainment* at provincial one-night stands until 1861. When the sketch was revived for the sisters' Benefit at the Theatre Royal, Bristol, E. W. Godwin wrote in *The Western Daily Press* on 1st December, 1863:

> The make-up of Mrs Terrorbody, and the free-hearted jollity of Hector . . . were perhaps unimprovable. Hector's foot action, which I have heard shallow critics blame, is not only natural to Miss Ellen Terry, but would have been equally so to the laughter-loving pupil of old Jollyboy.

Kate and her father had joined the stock company at the Theatre Royal, Bristol for the 1861 autumn season while Ellen remained in London with Madame Albina de Rhona's company at the New Royalty. Ellen's first role — Clementine in Eugene Sue's *Atar Gull* — attracted the audience's attention immediately. *The Atheneum* recorded:

> Miss Ellen Terry . . . acted with interesting naiveté and had a situation of some difficulty to realise. She is attacked in a summer house, the door of which is locked, by a large serpent, and forces her way out of the window, with the coils about her neck, shrieking with terror. The young lady depicted this fearful incident so naturally that she deservedly obtained very great applause.

Ellen had her hair cut unusually short in 1859 in order to play the part of Hector in *Home for the Holiday* by W. T. Moncrieff. Kate played her stage sister and the two were photographed by Walter Lacy when they were appearing at Ryde on the Isle of Wight.

The season at the New Royalty was not a success, however, and Ellen spent much of the first half of 1862 at home. When Kate returned from Bristol Tom Taylor suggested that she would make an ideal model for the painter G. F. Watts. Ellen accompanied Kate to the artist's studio and Watts, on seeing them both, decided to create a double portrait. Not surprisingly, Ellen emerged as the dominant figure.

In the autumn of 1862 Ellen joined Kate in Bristol, making her debut as Cupid in the burlesque *Endymion* by William Brough. The reviewer on *The Bristol Mercury* was smitten immediately: ''We could believe anything about head-turning and heart-sickening were Love always to present himself in the guise of Miss Ellen Terry.''

E. W. Godwin tempered his praise with more astute criticism as always and in *The Western Daily Press* on 30th October, 1862, he wrote:

> The younger Miss Terry's winning manner almost makes one ashamed to find fault, but some people would prefer to see Cupid standing occasionally on more than one leg, and not always smiling.

Laura Taylor's watercolour sketch of Kate as Beatrice and Ellen as Hero in *Much Ado About Nothing* at the Theatre Royal, Haymarket, 1863.

Far left: William Brough's burlesque, *Endymion*, 1862: Henrietta Hodson in the title role, with Kate as Diana and Ellen as Cupid (in the daring costume she is alleged to have worn off-stage at parties). Photograph by H. N. King. *Left: The Little Treasure* by Harris and Williams, 1862. Photograph by Herbert Watkins.

Ellen first met Godwin in Bristol when she and Kate took part in Shakespeare readings at his house. Godwin later designed a dress for Ellen to wear as Titania in a production of *A Midsummer Night's Dream* mounted to open the new Theatre Royal in Bath in March, 1863. The theatre management, unfortunately, considered the costume too unconventional and Ellen was not allowed to wear it on stage.

At the end of March, 1863, Kate returned to London to join Charles Fechter at the Lyceum Theatre and Ellen joined John Buckstone's company at the Haymarket. E. L. Blanchard saw Ellen as Gertrude Howard in *The Little Treasure* by Harris and Williams:

> She is very young, but shows no trace of immaturity either in her style or figure. Tall for her age, of prepossessing appearance, and with expressive features full of vivacity and intelligence, she secured at once the sympathies of her audience, and retained them by the joyous spirit and deep feeling with which she imbued the personation. In the girlish playfulness exhibited through the first act Miss Ellen Terry was especially happy, and in characters illustrative of a frank and impulsive temperament the young actress will prove a most desirable addition to the feminine strength of the dramatic corps.

From this rapturous account it is easy to see why it was that during this season Ellen established herself as London's brightest ingénue. She also appeared as Hero in *Much Ado About Nothing* to Louisa Angell's Beatrice and played opposite Kate's Beatrice in Bristol too, but was soon back at the Haymarket.

Ellen was later to regard this engagement as ''one of my lost opportunities.'' The reason? The presence in Sheridan's *The Rivals* of J. B. Buckstone, W. H. Chippendale, Henry Compton and William Farren — all steeped in the traditions of Sheridan's own theatre. Together they must have been a rather fruity bunch who probably regarded a buxom fifteen-year-old as fair game for teasing. Ellen, like many practical jokers, did not care to be on the receiving end. In any case, she:

> . . . was just dreaming of and aspiring after another world, a world full of pictures and music and gentle, artistic people with quiet voices and elegant manners. The reality of such a world was Little Holland House, the house of Mr Watts.

Playwright Tom Taylor introduced Kate and Ellen Terry to George Frederick Watts, who painted this delightful double portrait of 'The Sisters' in 1862.

2. G. F. Watts

GEORGE FREDERICK WATTS married Ellen Terry on 20th February, 1864 at St. Barnabas' Church, Kensington. He was nearly forty-seven and she was not yet seventeen. Tom Taylor announced the wedding plans at a *Punch* dinner on 17th February and one of the company, Henry Silver, noted in his diary:

> . . . apropos of old Watts marrying Miss Ellen Terry — who really loves him. She receives as a Valentine the ashes of her photographs burnt by an admirer . . .

It is generally believed that the wedding was arranged by Tom Taylor and Mrs Thoby Prinsep in whose home, Little Holland House, Watts had been installed as 'artistic genius in residence'. But even if they had a hand in the final arrangements, Watts had had some very definite ideas of his own on Ellen as early as 1862, when Lady Constance Leslie received an unusual letter from him:

> Knowing how much you are interested in the Miss Terrys I am going to tell you a thing that will perhaps surprise you. I have determined to remove the youngest from the temptations and abominations of the Stage, give her an education and if she continues to have the affection she now feels for me, marry her. There is a great difference between her age and mine and I shall not think of putting any pressure upon her inclinations, but I think whatever the future brings, I can hardly regret taking the poor child out of her present life and fitting her for a better. I hope in what I have undertaken to do, I shall have the countenance of my friends, for it is no light matter from any point of view. Even the expense will be considerable, as I shall have to compensate her family for the loss of her services. If you and any others, whose opinion may be valued, think well of my object, I would be very glad if you would tell Mrs Prinsep and her family, for you know the prejudice that is against the Stage. (I have it myself.) Miss Terry is

Portrait of Ellen by Mary Anne Hall, 1866.

very young and I do not see the future at all distinctly but giving her a chance of qualifying herself for a good position in true Society I do not think I ought to be thought ill of.

Clearly the relationship was doomed from the start. For as W. Graham Robertson observed in a letter to Kerrison Preston, written on 9th January, 1939: "If Watts thought he could mould that vital and radiant creature into what he wished her to be, he did not show much intelligence."

A. M. W. Stirling heard that Watts had thought of *adopting* Ellen. Indeed, he did adopt two ten-year-old girls: Blanche Clogstoun in 1861 and Lillian MacKintosh in 1889. Ellen herself seems to suggest that there was a more mundane reason for the hastily arranged marriage. On 7th November, 1896 she wrote to George Bernard Shaw:

> I'll never forget my first kiss. I made myself such a donkey over it, and always laugh now when I remember. Mr Watts kissed me in the studio one day, but sweetly and gently, all tenderness and kindness, and then I was what they called 'engaged' to him and all the rest of it, and my people hated it, and I was in heaven for I knew I was to live with those pictures. 'Always' I thought, and to sit to that gentle Mr W. and clean his brushes, and play my idiotic piano to him, and sit with him there in wonderland [the studio].

Julia Margaret Cameron had only just started to use a camera when she took these portraits of Ellen and Watts in 1864. She depicted Ellen as 'The South West Wind' but captured Watts in a more straight-forward manner — resting on the balcony of the house in Cromwell Place belonging to the painter and founder of the Pre-Raphaelite Brotherhood, Sir John Everett Millais.

'Choosing' by Watts, 1864. W. Graham Robertson wrote to congratulate his friend Kerrison Preston on his purchase of the portrait in 1934: "It is a picture with a special intimate quality . . . . it actually holds the wistful soul of Ellen Terry and is, in a way, prophetic of her life; she spent nearly all her days trying to persuade herself that there was scent in camellias, while the perfume really came from the hidden violets near her heart."

Julia Margaret Cameron was always trying out unusual poses and locations for her long-suffering sitters. Ellen and Watts spent their honeymoon at her home on the Isle of Wight and one morning, as dawn broke, she rushed Ellen across the fields (still in her chemise) to Tennyson's house where she had earlier spotted a suitable background for a portrait — in the bathroom. In spite of some heavy re-touching (centre bottom and on Ellen's wrist, just above the bracelets) the result was one of the finest photographs of the Victorian era. Mrs Cameron must have been aware of Ellen's situation for she entitled the portrait 'Sadness'.

Ellen in her going-away outfit, 1864. Photograph by Elliott & Fry.

Then I got ill and had to stay at Little Holland House — and then — he kissed me — differently — not much differently but a little, and I told no-one for a fortnight, but when I was alone with Mother one day she looked so pretty and sad and kind, I told her — what do you think I told the poor darling? I told her I must be married to him now because I was going to have a baby!!! and she believed me!! Oh, I tell you I thought I knew everything then, but I was nearly 16 [*sic*] years old then — I was sure *that* kiss meant giving me a baby!

It is possible that Watts had originally envisaged a vaguely platonic Pygmalion/Galatea relationship though he knew that he might not succeed in wooing Ellen away from the stage, even after marriage. And there is a hint of this doubt in the title that he gave to his first formal portrait of her: *Choosing*. The painting must have been completed shortly after the wedding for it was shown at that year's Royal Academy exhibition.

Inside the studio things went well. Watts might have absent-mindedly caused Ellen to pause for so long in armour for *Joan of Arc* (the original title of *Watchman*) that she fainted, but otherwise their 'professional' relationship was fruitful. But elsewhere matters were more difficult. At Freshwater on the Isle of Wight, where the Prinseps had a holiday home near the house of the photographer Julia Margaret Cameron, Ellen was lonely. The only adult she spoke to at any length was another neighbour, Alfred Tennyson. Ellen later wrote:

I sat shrinking and timid, in a corner — the girl-wife of a famous painter. I was, if I was anything at all, more of a curiosity, a side show . . .

There are wild reports of Ellen running about in her 'outrageously revealing' Cupid dress, dancing naked on bishops' dinner tables, and letting her hair down (literally) in front of visitors. But A. M. W. Stirling's account rings truer:

Incompatible as was such a union between Watts with his serious aims and high spiritual ideals and a lovely, wayward child whose undeveloped genius was of a totally different order, my uncle always said that the person who wrecked the marriage was Mrs Prinsep. She never ceased to treat Ellen as a naughty child who must be scolded and made obedient, and a high-spirited, unconventional girl naturally resented this treatment, while Watts, absorbed in his art, was little aware of the mischief which was preparing.

Watts did not succeed in introducing Ellen into Society as he had wished. Henry Silver attended a *Punch* dinner on 12th June, 1867 and afterwards recorded in his diary:

> We talk of the sad position of Ellen Terry . . . whom Watts has left with £300.00 a year . . . . Mrs Prinsep snubbed the wife, and the husband like a coward did not defend her. Kicky [George du Maurier] is savage against snubs in High Life inviting a husband without a wife . . .

When Ellen realised what was happening she refused at first to agree to a separation but the relationship was formally terminated on 26th January, 1865. The marriage had lasted for less than a year. Ellen met Watts only once again, in Brighton in 1872. Watts saw Ellen on stage at the Lyceum in *Hamlet* in 1878-79 and sent her an early portrait and a sketch from a photograph. He also re-worked a painting of her as Ophelia. After that the couple corresponded until Watts married again in 1886.

After the separation Ellen returned to her parents. And it was at their house in Kentish Town that Lewis Carroll arrived on 21st December, 1864 to take photographs of the Terry family. He recorded in his diary that:

> Polly and Benjamin met me in the hall, and in the drawing room I found Miss Kate Terry, Florence, and to my delight, the one I have always most wished to meet of the family, Mrs Watts . . . . I was very pleased with what I saw of Mrs Watts — lively and pleasant, almost childish in her fun, but perfectly lady-like. Her sister [Kate] seemed ill and out of spirits. I fancy her gaiety yesterday, and Mrs Watts' today, were both partly assumed.

Not unnaturally, Ellen appears to have been badly shaken by her failed marriage, and as late as 10th August, 1865 William Allingham heard of her when he stayed at the Sun Inn in Lymington on the Isle of Wight and spotted a portrait of her on the wall:

> I say to the girl who waits [the landlady's daughter], 'I know who that is.' She says to me 'Yes, it's Mrs Watts — she's staying here', which much surprised me. It seems she used to put up there in old times when playing at the Ryde Theatre, and now, being married — and separated — she goes about by herself from place to place, and has come for a while to her friendly old quarters.

Lewis Carroll photographed members of the Terry family on several occasions. *Left:* Ellen and Florence, 1864. *Right:* Ellen in January, 1865. She displays more of the wedding dress and the Indian shawl she wore with it than Watts included in 'Choosing'.

Members of the famous Punch clique assembled in costume for the production of a double bill consisting of Tom Taylor's *A Sheep in Wolf's Clothing* and the premiere of Arthur Sullivan's first opera, *Cox and Box*, at a Benefit performance for the widow of the Punch illustrator C. H. Bennett at the Adelphi Theatre, 11th May, 1867. The photograph was taken at the studio of the London Stereoscopic Company. *From left to right, standing:* R. T. Pritchett; Shirley Brooks; Arthur Lewis; Mark Lemon; Quentin Twiss; John Tenniel; Arthur Blunt; Henry Silver. *From left to right, seated:* Arthur Sullivan; Ellen; George du Maurier; Kate Terry; Tom Taylor. Also in the company but not present for the photograph: F. C. Burnand; Florence Terry; Miss Stoker.

On 20th June, 1866 Ellen returned to the stage for a Benefit held for her sister Kate and in May 1867 she took part in a *Punch* clique benefit matinée. In October of the same year she appeared at Kate's farewell performances. All presumably were unpaid. Ellen did not actually need to return to work for Watts continued to pay her an allowance, though only on condition that she did not go on the stage. But her parents — and Tom Taylor — felt that she would be much happier if she started acting again so she joined the company being assembled by Charles Reade for the opening of the New Queen's Theatre, Holborn.

Ellen's first appearance for Reade was in his own play, *The Double Marriage*. During the run her proneness to corpsing and camping it up were much in evidence:

> There was one 'curtain' which used to convulse [Charles] Wyndham. He had a line, 'Whose child is this?' and there was I, looking a mere child myself, and with a bad cold in my head too answering 'It's bine!' The very thought of it used to send us off into fits of laughter — on stage.

On a particularly foggy Boxing Night Ellen appeared for the first time with Henry Irving in David Garrick's *Katherine and Petruchio*, in which she gave the first of her unconventional readings of a virago part; she presented Katherine as a spoilt child rather than a confirmed vixen. Irving thought she was too hoydenish. Her opinion of him was that he was "stiff with self-consciousness."

Their relative positions as star box-office attractions may be judged by their salaries for this engagement: Irving received £2.13s.4d. for his efforts while Ellen was paid £5. She was rapidly establishing herself as one of the leading actresses of her day when she decided, once again, to give up the stage.

The playbill for Ellen's first appearance with Henry Irving in *Katherine and Petruchio*, 1867, David Garrick's version of *The Taming of the Shrew*.

Ellen's own caricature of herself in a letter to Kate, 1867.

THE NEW
QUEEN'S THEATRE,
LONG   ACRE.

Lessee and Manager,   Mr. ALFRED WIGAN,
(FORMERLY LESSEE OF THE OLYMPIC AND ST. JAMES'S THEATRES.)
Licensed by the Lord Chamberlain to Mr. ALFRED WIGAN, Actual & Responsible Manager, Charles St., Long Acre.

FIRST APPEARANCE of the POPULAR COMEDIAN,
Mr. J. L. TOOLE.

BOXING-NIGHT, DEC. 26th, 1867, AND EVERY EVENING,
The Performances will commence at SEVEN with SHAKESPEARE'S COMEDY of

KATHERINE
AND
PETRUCHIO.

Petruchio,   -   Mr. HENRY IRVING,
(His First Appearance at this Theatre).

Baptista,   -   Mr. W. H. STEPHENS,

Hortensio,   Mr. CRELLIN,   Grumio,   Mr. L. BROUGH,

Music Master,   Mr. SANGER,   Tailor,   Mr. C. SEYTON,

Biondello,   Mr. J. CLAYTON,

Pedro,   Mr. GEORGE,   Walter,   Mr. WOODFIELD,

Nathaniel,   Mr. J. VINCENT,

Gabriel,   Mr. BRAND,   Gregory,   Mr. MARTIN,

Adam,   Mr. WILSON,   Ralph,   Mr. FOTHERINGHAM,

Katherine,   -   Miss ELLEN TERRY,

Bianca,   Miss E. MAXSE,   Curtis,   Miss EVERARD,

3. E. W. Godwin

EDWARD WILLIAM GODWIN left Bristol shortly after his wife died in May 1864 and almost immediately established himself as a bright young architect in London. He had already found national fame with his design for the Guildhall, Northampton, and by 1867 he had secured other highly desirable commissions, most notably the complete design of the exterior, interior and furniture of Dromore Castle for the Earl of Limerick.

It has been suggested that Godwin renewed his acquaintance with Ellen at Little Holland House but it is also highly likely that they re-met in 1866 when he visited her backstage at the Queen's Theatre. Their relationship was obviously well advanced by 1868, for on 10th October Ellen left London and went to live with Godwin in a cottage in Hertfordshire. She had not told her parents where she was and when an unknown girl was found drowned Ben Terry identified the body as his daughter. Sarah, however, thought otherwise and Ellen had to make an appearance to prove her correct.

Whether Ellen told her parents exactly where she was living is not clear. When Lewis Carroll called on the family on 9th April, 1869 he was told that, "Mrs Watts is still staying in lodgings . . ." By this time, in fact, Ellen was expecting her first baby. A daughter, Edith (Edy), was born on 9th December.

On 16th January, 1872 Edward (Teddy) was born, not at the cottage but at the house of the midwife in Stevenage. Godwin did not register the birth but Ellen did. Characteristically ignoring the caution: "Any person who falsifies any of the particulars on this certificate is liable to prosecution", she boldly declared her name to be Eleanor Alice Godwin, née Watkins (i.e. the 'kin of Watts').

Godwin designed a new house for his family — 'Fallows Green' at Harpenden. They went to London seldom, took their holidays in Normandy and were blissfully happy leading a country life. Ellen clearly saw herself as living in a sort of Helen Allingham/Kate Greenaway picture-book world. Her two children had an exceptional upbringing in this 'aesthetic' household. They were allowed only well-designed story-books and wooden toys, and Japanese prints and fans

Ellen at the time of her association with E. W. Godwin. She is displaying a particularly fine range of 'ethnic' and 'classical' jewellery (probably purchased at Liberty's) as well as her favourite long jade necklace, which set the fashion for 'Bohemian' women for several generations. Photograph by Herbert Watkins, 1872.

'Fallows Green', the house (now demolished) near Harpenden in Hertfordshire designed by Godwin. He lived there with Ellen and their two children, Edy and Teddy, from 1870-73. An anonymous line engraving after a painting by Johnston Forbes-Robertson.

lined the nursery walls. And woe betide any well-meaning friend who brought the wrong kind of gift. Edy was so well trained that she immediately denounced as vulgar a doll dressed in shocking pink silk that she had been given.

Needless to say, the country idyll could not last. Godwin and his business partner became involved in a legal dispute about their practice, customers threatened to sue when charges exceeded estimates and as a consequence 'Fallows Green' had to be mortgaged.

In spite of these financial difficulties Ellen never considered returning to the stage until, in a manner worthy of one of his plays, Charles Reade once more entered her life. It was January 1874:

> One day I was driving in a narrow lane, when the wheel of my pony cart came off. I was standing there, thinking what I should do next, when a whole crowd of horsemen in 'pink' came leaping over the hedge into the lane. One of them stopped and asked if he could do anything. Then he looked hard at me and exclaimed: 'Good God! It's Nelly!'. The man was Charles Reade.

Reade asked her if she had thought of going back to work and she explained that she had been living a contented life in the country, but then:

> I remembered the bailiff in the house . . . and said laughingly: 'Well, perhaps I would think of it if someone would give me forty pounds a week!' 'Done,' said Charles Reade, 'I'll give you that, and more, if you'll come and play Philippa Chester in *The Wandering Heir*.

So Ellen accepted. But she always looked back on those six years in the country with great nostalgia and continued to re-create the way of life she had so enjoyed by buying a succession of cottages before settling finally in Smallhythe in Kent.

Although Ellen was to marry twice again, it is generally considered that Godwin was the man who brought her the most joy. W. Graham Robertson summed the relationship up well:

> Though I know most people would not think so, Ellen Terry was a 'one man' woman. She loved (in the true sense of the word) one man only — and for ever.

Godwin made this sketch of Ellen with curling-papers in her hair around 1870. It is inscribed 'Before' so there must have been a companion piece labelled 'After' to go with it.

4. Return to the Stage

JOHNSTON FORBES-ROBERTSON first met Ellen at her Taviton Street house in London in 1874. Forbes-Robertson was a fellow actor but he was also a painter and was interested in Ellen as a subject for a portrait. He was totally charmed:

> I was ushered into the drawing room, the decorations of which, for those days, were very novel and bizarre. The curtains were of a pale blue Japanese pattern in cretonne. There was a dado of matting, matting covered the floor, and the few chairs that were in the rooms were of bamboo. In the centre of the room was a full-sized cast of the Venus de Milo, on a pedestal about three feet high, on the ledge of which was a censer in which incense was burning, the tapering clouds of which spiralled round the noble form of the statue. Into the back part of this blue and yellow room floated surely a wraith, for the attenuated and beautifully proportioned figure before me was wrapped in a light blue kimono, and thus, with her pale face and yellow hair, free and flowing, she melted into the surroundings. But presently this wraith materialised, and welcomed me with outstretched hands. The ethereal creature looked more like eighteen or twenty than twenty-six, and in manner — well, she was just a girl, and indeed this youthful buoyant spirit she maintained all through her life, infecting with it all those who came into contact with her.

When Ellen took over the role of Philippa Chester from Mrs John Wood in *The Wandering Heir* on 28th February, 1874 she met with a tremendous reception. All the old impishness was still there, as Forbes-Robertson recorded:

> Charles Kelly was the 'villain' of the piece, and in the final scene, when his roguery was unmasked and his disguise wig snatched from his head and thrown on the

Godwin was one of the earliest admirers of Japanese arts and crafts in the West and Samuel Walker caught Ellen in a very relaxed mood wearing a blue kimono (incorrectly adjusted) in 1874.

Left: Ellen as Philippa Chester in Charles Reade's *The Wandering Heir,* the role that marked her return to the stage on 28th February, 1874. Photograph by the London Stereoscopic Company. *Centre:* As Portia in Squire Bancroft's production of *The Merchant of Venice* at the Prince of Wales Theatre, 1875. This splendid gown, designed for her by Godwin, was made of a heavy brocade in the then newly fashionable colours of Wedgwood blue and white. The book she is holding was not real but was a stage prop specially created by Godwin. Photograph by Fradelle & Young. *Right:* As Portia disguised as Balthazar in *The Merchant of Venice,* 1875.

ground, she often delighted, much to the rage and disgust of Kelly, in sliding on it when rushing into my arms. The more sulky he grew, the more she took pleasure in baiting him.

Dion Boucicault wanted to take Ellen to America but Reade persuaded her to stay and re-build her London and provincial reputation gradually. For the next few months she toured successfully with Reade's company until she received an offer to play what was to become always her role — Portia in *The Merchant of Venice.* This particular production was mounted by the Bancrofts. Unfortunately, cast in the role of Shylock was Charles Coghlan whose performance was, in Ellen's own memorable phrase ''. . . not even bad. It was nothing.''

The character of Portia had usually been played either as a tragedy queen or as a soubrette until Ellen took over the part and tried to present her as the Renaissance woman that Shakespeare had envisaged. *The Daily Telegraph* of 19th April, 1875 acknowledged her efforts:

> They will say it was not Portia because it was perhaps like no other Portia ever seen by Shakespeare students, so fresh and charming is the representation . . . no renewal of old business . . . Miss Terry, in her beautiful robes, looked as if she had stepped out of a canvas by Mr Leighton.

The production, however, was a box-office flop, though Ellen's reputation was assured and her audiences more admiring than ever. For

the first time in her experience, she declared, she felt like a conqueror on stage. After Portia she played several other roles for the rest of the season, though none with such great success. Shaw claimed, of her performance in *Ours* by T. W. Robertson in May 1876: ''She left an impression of waywardness: of not quite fitting into her part and not wanting to.''

Ellen's presence in the Bancrofts' company was not always comfortable. During one performance she managed to stab Mrs Bancroft and there were rumours that it was not merely an accident. Obviously she had much to worry her. Godwin had finally left her just before *The Merchant of Venice* opened but he continued to cause her anxiety. In a letter to a Mr Wilson she wrote:

> In all gentleness and kindness of feeling, I must beg you
> not to act as mediator between Mr Godwin and myself.
> Our separation was a thing agreed upon by both of us
> many weeks before it actually took place. The first steps
> were taken by him and I am certainly much astonished
> to hear that he professes any strong feeling in the
> matter. Part of our compact was that we should always
> maintain a kindly, friendly relation to one another —
> He has since Tuesday last made this an *impossibility*. He
> tried by unfair means to get my little girl from me (I had
> offered to let him have the boy) and I now distinctly
> refuse to hold any communication whatever with him.

In January 1876 Godwin married Beatrice Phillips. Ellen subsequently relied on Tom Taylor and Charles Reade for advice and support. It may have been at their suggestion that Watts started divorce proceedings in March 1877, on the grounds of Ellen's adultery with Godwin.

Ellen joined John Hare's company in November 1876, at the Court Theatre, and in December she had a major success in Tom Taylor's *New Men for Old Acres* in which she played opposite Charles Kelly again. When Lewis Carroll saw her on 16th January, 1877 he recorded in his diary that Ellen:

> . . . was wonderful and I should think unsurpassable in
> all but the lighter parts. The gush of animal spirits of a
> light-hearted girl is beyond her now, poor thing! She
> can give a clever imitation of it, but that is all.

Ellen was, of course, thirty years old by now. The play was a hit but not everyone was impressed. Henry James's adverse review in *The Galaxy* (May 1877) does, however, like Shaw's 'attacks' on Irving, give a clearer view of Ellen in action than many more favourable but less considered commentaries:

Miss Ellen Terry . . . is usually spoken of by the 'refined' portion of the public as the most interesting actress in London. Miss Terry is picturesque; she looks like a pre-Raphaelitish drawing in a magazine — the portrait of the crop-haired heroine in the illustration to the series novel. She is intelligent and vivacious, and she is indeed, in a certain measure, interesting. With great frankness and spontaneity, she is at the same time singularly delicate and lady-like, and it seems almost impertinent to criticise her harshly. But the favour which Miss Terry enjoys strikes me, like that under which Mr Irving has expanded, as a sort of measure of the English critical sense in things theatrical. Miss Terry has all the pleasing qualities I have enumerated, but she has, with them, the defect that she is simply not an actress. One sees it sufficiently in her face — the face of a clever young English woman, with a hundred merits, but not that of a dramatic artist.

In June 1877 *School for Scandal* was revived with Ellen as Lady Teazle and Kelly as Sir Peter. And it was during the run of Lord Lytton's *The House of Darnley* — on 21st November (a fortnight after her divorce from Watts became absolute) — that Ellen was married to Charles Kelly, in a service conducted by his father, a clergyman. Ellen was reconciled with her parents, and her children adopted Kelly's real surname of Wardell.

It was not long, however, before the first signs of professional jealousy began to appear. John Hare decided to stage *Olivia*, an adaptation of Oliver Goldsmith's *The Vicar of Wakefield*, with Ellen in the title role. Kelly was offered the part of Burchell (which would have suited his 'bulldog' personality) but he wanted to play the Vicar (which would not). He did not appear, therefore, in the big hit of the season. The critic Clement Scott analysed the play's success:

[Hare] . . . wanted an English play, on an English subject, with an English setting . . . . A happier idea could not have occurred to mortal man. We were in the middle of a seventeenth [*sic*] century craze. We were all mad about blue china, Chippendale chairs, Sheraton sideboards, old spinets, and brass fire-irons. George du Maurier with his 'Punch' pictures had started the fashion, and there was scarcely one in the artistic world who did not in their own home and belongings revert with joy to the modes and whims of their great-grandmothers.

Indeed, it could be said that the success of *Olivia* was greatly increased by the scenery and costumes, which were designed by Marcus Stone RA, who specialised in paintings of eighteenth-century life. London went 'Olivia' mad. Edgar Pemberton described the phenomenon:

> No wonder that this fascinating Olivia became the rage of the day. Her photographs went like wildfire; the milliners' windows were full of Olivia hats, caps, 'kerchiefs and other items of feminine adornment; everywhere such dainty trifles were in evidence; and how many little 'Olivias' were christened in 1878 would be hard to say.

Lewis Carroll was again impressed by Ellen's acting when he saw the production on 22nd April: "[She acted] with a sweetness and pathos that moved some of the audience (nearly including myself) to tears." The distinguished Shakespearean producer William Poel was less enthusiastic, however: "[Her] acting is graceful but she quite failed through lack of voice to make her part impressive." Dutton Cook, on the other hand, claimed that: "Prettier pictures have not indeed been seen upon the stage than are afforded by the Primrose family, their friends and neighbours, goods and chattels and general surroundings.''

Henry James, scathing as usual, declared (in *The Nation*, 13th June, 1878) that *Olivia's* success:

> . . . could only be accounted for by the extraordinary apathy of taste on the part of the public, and a good-natured disposition in the well-fed British play goer who sits in the stalls after dinner to accept a pretty collection of eighteenth century chairs, and buffets, and pottery . . . as a substitute for dramatic composition and finished acting.

Again Henry James contrasted Ellen's 'amateurishness' with French acting skill but had to admit nevertheless that: ''Miss Ellen Terry, whom it is greatly the fashion to admire, has a great deal of charm, and an interesting, pathetic, even beautiful countenance.'' Even he had to acknowledge that her reputation was by now too well-established to be damaged by anything that he had to say.

Meanwhile, Henry Irving, London's foremost younger actor, had been enjoying a popular season at the Lyceum Theatre in the Strand, and at the end of 1878 he took the opportunity to take over the lease. He had already started to form his own company in the summer and was looking for a new leading lady to replace Isobel Bateman, daughter of his current manager, Mrs H. L. Bateman. Lady Pollock suggested Ellen Terry and Irving contacted her. Ellen wrote to him on 19th July, saying: ''I shall be pleased indeed if you will call any day this or next week . . . (any day but next Tuesday or Monday) . . .'' Irving replied immediately: ''I look forward to the pleasure of calling upon you on Tuesday next at two o'clock.'' And so began the most famous stage partnership of the century.

5. Irving and the Lyceum

HENRY IRVING left his meeting with Ellen Terry convinced that he had made her a definite offer. In a letter to his old schoolmaster, Dr Pinches, he outlined the financial and organisational aspects of taking over the Lyceum and added: "I have engaged Ellen Terry — not a bad start — eh?"

Ellen, however, was not clear that anything definite had been agreed. She wrote from Liverpool on 25th August: "If you will write to me . . . making me some definite proposition, I will answer you definitely." Eventually the initial terms were agreed. Ellen would receive £40 per week plus half the proceeds (after expenses had been deducted) of a benefit each season.

Irving decided to open his first season in 1879 with *Hamlet*. He already knew the play well, having played Laertes opposite both Charles Fechter and Edwin Booth, who were, respectively, the leading British and American Hamlets of the 1860's. Although Irving had played Hamlet at the Lyceum under Mrs Bateman in 1874, this new production would give him a chance to stamp his own personality completely on the role.

Alan Hughes has analysed Irving's genius as a director and actor and has come to the conclusion that his original and controversial interpretations are still valid today:

> He was determined to show what every word meant rather than to recite beautiful sounds. Inevitably his own part was over-emphasised by omissions, simplifications and the sheer focussing power of his genius, but the production was probably not as over-simplified as most we see today.

When rehearsals for *Hamlet* began Ellen was very much the newcomer. Most actors in Irving's company had worked together before and knew their parts well. Ellen put in even more preparation than usual for her role as Ophelia, which she had never tackled, and she was understandably dismayed when Irving gave sensational read-throughs of all the parts — except hers, which he glossed over.

'Ellen Terry': lithograph by William Rothenstein, 1897.

Ellen and Henry as Ophelia and Hamlet (1878), in an engraving by Edward H.
Bell.

"My lord, I have remembrances of yours,
That I have longed long to re-deliver;
I pray you, now receive them."

Act III, Scene i

Watts continued to follow Ellen's career after their divorce. When she opened as Ophelia at the Lyceum he sent her this pencil drawing (*left*) that he had made from a photograph (*right*) taken by Window & Grove.

Irving continued to ignore her until ten days before the opening when Ellen plucked up enough courage to ask him when they were going to rehearse their scenes together. He replied, ''We shall be all right!'' And of course they were.

They did discuss the costumes as both were interested in historical authenticity. Ellen discovered (from Godwin) that the correct colour for mourning dress in medieval Denmark was red but decided that this was perhaps a bit too strident so had a black dress made for the Mad Scene. She explained all this to Irving one morning. He listened patiently and then politely dismissed her for the time being. The next day she received a visit from Walter Lacy, Irving's costume adviser, who had been sent to suggest that in *Hamlet* only one character was allowed to wear black. Ellen's costume was re-made in the traditional virginal white.

Hamlet ran for 108 nights and Lewis Carroll summed up the general opinion: ''Irving rather spoiled Hamlet by his extraordinary English. Ellen Terry as Ophelia was simply perfect.''

Ellen's other roles during that first season were also in revivals of existing Lyceum productions, but some critics thought that her modern naturalistic technique did not suit the old plays where they had been accustomed to Irving's studied approach. Her tendency to 'humanise' unsympathetic characters gave rise to comment too. *The Daily News* reviewed *The Lady of Lyons*, in which Ellen played Pauline, on 18th April, 1879:

Those who are fortunate enough to have seen this actress's performance in . . . "Olivia" cannot have forgotten the terrible power of her expression of hatred and aversion for the man who had so basely betrayed a trusting nature. If, therefore, Miss Terry chooses to moderate those fierce denunciatory tones, to soften down those bitter sarcasms and angry taunts which it has been customary rather to colour highly than to subdue, she will not be suspected of falling short on the occasion from any lack of means. She chooses, apparently, rather to exhibit the love of the woman still struggling to show itself in spite of the cruel fraud of which she is the victim, and to appear crushed for a while by a sensitive woman's dread of the mockery of idle tongues, rather than moved by fierce resentment towards her betrayer. All this is very beautiful, and the inexpressible grace of all her movements and attitudes, the perfect simplicity, truth and directness of all her utterances, add to the performance of a singular charm. Yet it must be confessed that nature portrayed so moderately and with so much sweetness and truth is a little out of keeping with the somewhat artificial character of the play.

In 1899 Edward Gordon Craig published a portfolio of woodcuts entitled 'Henry Irving, Ellen Terry'. This one is called 'Miss Ellen Terry's Dressing-room'.

Ellen's first season was rounded off by revivals of two plays by W. G. Wills; in one of Irving's tours de force, *Eugene Aram*, she had the minor part of Ruth Meadows, but in *Charles I* she played Queen Henrietta Maria, which had been one of Miss Bateman's roles. Here she was allowed to demonstrate her facility to cry to order. William Archer was told by Henry Howe:

> I have often shed tears in sympathetic situations, especially when aided by the sensibility of the artist who is acting with me. For instance, in the last act of *Charles I* when Huntley leads the children to their mother I invariably shed tears at the point where Miss Terry, also with tears in her eyes, asks Huntley if the children know of their father's fate. Again, when the King takes leave of Huntley, previous to going to execution Mr Irving copiously sheds tears . . . . I have often been told by those who have witnessed the scene that there was scarcely a dry eye in the house.

During the summer break Ellen toured the provinces with Kelly, returning to the Lyceum for *Hamlet* and rehearsals for Irving's new production of *The Merchant of Venice*. Irving and his designers strove to re-create the Venice of Veronese exactly as the Bancrofts did in 1875.

'Miss Ellen Terry as Ophelia': a coloured woodcut by Edward Gordon Craig and his first published illustration, 1898.

This engraving by W. H. Margetson was made from Hawes Craven's careful re-creation of Frederick Goodall's popular painting 'The Happy Days of Charles I'. It was issued as a souvenir of the 1892 revival of W. G. Wills' *Charles I* and shows the finale to Act I, with the Royal Family setting off for a journey down-river on the Royal Barge from the gardens near Hampton Court. *From left to right:* William Terriss as Lord Moray; Minnie Terry (Ellen's niece) as Princess Elizabeth; Miss Webb as Prince James; Henry Irving as Charles I; Ellen as Queen Henrietta Maria.

Ellen as Queen Henrietta Maria in the 1879 production of *Charles I.*

> In the lone tent, waiting for victory,
>   She stands with eyes marred by the mists of pain,
>   Like some wan lily overdrenched with rain:
> The clamorous clang of arms, the ensanguined sky,
> War's ruin, and the wreck of chivalry
>   To her proud soul no common fear can bring:
>   Bravely she tarrieth for her Lord the King,
> Her soul a-flame with passionate ecstasy.
> O Hair of Gold! O Crimson Lips! O Face
>   Made for the luring and the love of man!
> With thee I do forget the toil and stress,
>   The loveless road that knows no resting place,
>   Time's straitened pulse, the soul's dread weariness,
> My freedom, and my life republican!
>
> Oscar Wilde: 'Queen Henrietta Maria'

But where their production had failed because of a weak Shylock, Irving's succeeded because of his striking reading of the character — not as the traditional villainous stage Jew figure of fun but as a fiercely proud Rothschild-like Jew and a symbol of a persecuted race. As a result, Ellen found that:

> Henry Irving's Shylock necessitated an entire revision of my conception of Portia, especially in the trial scene . . . . I had considered . . . that Portia in the trial scene ought to be very quiet. I saw an extraordinary effect in this quietness. But as Henry's Shylock was quiet, I had to give it up. His heroic saint was splendid, but it wasn't good for Portia.

The Merchant of Venice opened on 1st November, 1879 and was presented for 280 consecutive nights. It became the safe Irving/Terry

play in the Lyceum repertoire just as *The Bells* had been for Irving previously. Some nice journalistic controversies helped to keep the public interested. John Ruskin saw the production on 29th November; when he met Irving he praised the play but the next day he sent a rather critical letter, concentrating mainly on Ellen's Portia:

> . . . though Miss Terry's Portia has obtained so much applause, it greatly surprised me that you have not taught her a grander reading of the part. Portia is chiefly great in her majestic humility (the main sign of her splendid intellect) and — to take one instance of what I do not doubt to be misinterpretation — the speech, ''You see me Lord Bassanio . . . '' she would, I am certain, produce its true effect on the audience only if spoken with at least half a dozen yards between her and Bassanio — and with her eye on the ground through most of her lines.

By the time this letter arrived, however, Irving had already passed on Ruskin's original comments to *The Theatre*, a magazine he owned. These were published in January 1880 but by that time the nominal owner of the magazine was not Irving but Clement Scott. Ruskin objected and managed to persuade Scott to publish a correction. It was all fuel to the promotional fire.

Possibly more useful as free advertising was a scathing attack on Ellen's Portia in *Blackwood's Magazine*, which suggested that not only did she forget the importance of being earnest in the trial scene but that (worse still), when she urged Bassanio to tarry before trying his fortune with the caskets, ''. . . she holds him caressingly by the hand, nay, almost in an embrace, with all the unrestrained fondness which is conceivable only after he had actually won her.''

To mark the 100th night Irving held a five-course dinner for 350 guests on stage after the performance. He thus established a custom that became legendary and was to cost him a fortune. Max Beerbohm described one such glittering occasion:

> Everybody seemed to be standing on tip-toe, peering bright-eyed over heads, and everybody was talking at the top of his or her voice, and everybody's theme was composed of ''Henry'' and ''Ellen'' in about equal proportions. They all knew one another; and all, diverse though they were, were united in the bond of their hero-worship and heroine-worship . . . having abandoned all hope of setting eyes on my host, I was consoled by a vision of Miss Terry. Accompanied by three or four of the ardent and picturesque young ladies

The foyer of the Lyceum as it was in 1890. Around the box-office are originals of the drawings published in the souvenir programmes for *The Dead Heart, Macbeth* and *Ravenswood*. This area — along with the rest of the building in which Ellen and Irving worked — was completely demolished and replaced by a variety theatre in 1904.

I marvel not Bassanio was so bold
     To peril ail he had upon the lead,
     Or that proud Aragon bent low his head
Or that Morocco's fiery heart grew cold:
For in that gorgeous dress of beaten gold
     Which is more golden than the golden sun
     No woman Veronese looked upon
Was half so fair as thou whom I behold.
Yet fairer when with wisdom as your shield
     The sober-suited lawyer's gown you donned,
And would not let the laws of Venice yield
     Antonio's heart to that accursed Jew —
     O Portia! take my heart: it is thy due:
I think I will not quarrel with the Bond.

                    Oscar Wilde: 'Portia'

Ellen as Portia in the Lyceum
production of *The Merchant of
Venice*, 1883. Portrait by
G. W. Baldry.

who attach themselves to the suite of any very eminent actress, she was making her way down the narrow and crazy looking wooden staircase that led from the dressing-rooms to the stage. Half-way, she paused suddenly and clasped her hands up in front of her as she gazed down at the sea of bobbing heads. The gesture betokened a mingling of rapture and fear — the emotion of a wood-nymph about to take her first plunge in the sea . . . . I wondered what, at this moment, was passing through her bonny brain. Was the whole thing as fresh as ever to her? Did she really, as her mien indicated, feel herself half-allured, half-terrified, by the prospect of a plunge into waters unknown? Or had she, after all these years, become habituated, as to the morning bath?

The main events of the 1880-81 Lyceum season were productions of *The Cup, Othello* and *The Belle's Stratagem. The Cup* brought two figures from Ellen's past back into her life: Tennyson, who was the author of the play, and Godwin, who designed her costumes and the 'cup' itself. Henry Labouchaire explained in *The Truth* why the production was so well-timed:

I am inclined to consider Mr Irving a very practical, hard-headed man of business. He is one of those quiet people who appear to be led, but who invariably have their own way; and besides that, he inevitably understands the spirit of the age in which he lives. At a time of affected aestheticism, of rapture and intensity, of sad wall-paper and queer dadoes, what a stroke of diplomacy it was to engage Ellen Terry! This graceful and picturesque creature is the high priestess of the enthusiasts. She suits the dreams of the idealists. The age that gave us a Grosvenor Gallery must necessarily enjoy Ellen Terry, for she is the embodiment of the aspirations of modern art with her waving movements and skill in giving life to drapery; she is the actress of all others to harmonise with gold backgrounds and to lounge under blossoming apple trees.

Modern art in this context was not the Pre-Raphaelites, with whose models Ellen Terry has frequently been compared, but Frederick Leighton and Lawrence Alma-Tadema. Ellen was the quintessential 'Greek' ideal for these artists and their admirers.

Another admirer was Oscar Wilde, who, under Godwin's guidance, was beginning to espouse the Aesthetic cause in design and decoration

Sir Henry Irving (*centre*) and Ellen (*left*) greet distinguished guests at a Lyceum first night reception and stage supper. Drawing by J. H. Bacon from John R. Sims 'Living London', 1902.

Ellen as Camma in Tennyson's *The Cup*, 1881.

As one who poring on a Grecian urn
  Scans the fair shapes some Attic hand hath made,
  God with slim goddess, goodly man with maid,
And for their beauty's sake is loth to turn
And face the obvious day, must I not yearn
  For many a secret moon of indolent bliss,
  When in the midmost shrine of Artemis
I see thee standing, antique-limbed, and stern?
And yet — methinks I'd rather see thee play
  That serpent of old Nile, whose witchery
Made Emperors drunken, — come, great Egypt, shake
  Our stage with all thy mimic pageants! Nay,
  I am grown sick of unreal passions, make
Thy world thine Actium, me thine Antony!

Oscar Wilde: 'Camma'

'The Private View at the Royal Academy, 1881' by William Powell Frith. Oscar Wilde is the prominent figure in a top hat to the right of centre. He is holding a catalogue and has an orchid in his lapel. Ellen and Irving are just visible behind his left shoulder.

Ellen in the nightgown she wore for the final scene as Desdemona in *Othello*, 1881. Photograph by Window & Grove.

Ellen and Henry were popular targets for the caricaturist Alfred Bryan. The "certain flatness at the end of her nose" is emphasised in his drawing of Ellen as Juliet in 1882 (*left*) and he had great fun satirising the minuet (*right*) featured in *The Belle's Stratagem* by Hannah Cowley. (Fred Vokes was the senior member of a family of pantomime artists prominent in London at the time.)

MISS ELLEN TERRY.

THE COMING JULIET.

NOW THAT MR. HENRY IRVING HAS TAKEN TO DANCING, MR. FRED VOKES MUST LOOK TO HIS LAURELS.

with considerable enthusiasm. He sent a typical first-night letter with some flowers:

> I write to wish you every success tonight. You could not do anything that would not be a mirror of the highest artistic beauty, and I am so glad to hear you have an opportunity of showing us that passionate power which I know you have . . .

James Wedmore wrote a glowing review of Ellen's performance:

> Under her thin, sea-green raiment of lissome stuff, the movement and arrested movement of the actress are equally perfect. Aided by draperies arranged with the most singular skill, the figure, in its freedom and suavity recalls the Elgin Marbles and the designs of the artist who has learnt the best use from them — Mr Albert Moore. In hue and line the actress is a realisation of Mr Moore's paintings.

As it was a short piece *The Cup* was played in a double bill with a revival of *The Corsican Brothers*, which had opened in September. This created even more work than usual for the stage-hands but it gave the audiences value for money for they were able to see Irving in three roles on one night (the Corsican twins being two parts in one, as it were).

For his production of *Othello* Irving engaged the American actor Edwin Booth, who had been having an unsuccessful winter season at the Princess's Theatre. Irving and Booth alternated as Othello and Iago, with Ellen as Desdemona.

By the beginning of 1881, however, Ellen's private life was having an adverse effect on her performances, for Kelly had left her. She went on her first Lyceum tour of the provinces during the summer and autumn and when the company returned to London at Christmas preparations were well advanced for the spring season.

Romeo and Juliet opened on 8th March, 1882 but although the production was visually stunning it was generally felt that neither Irving nor Ellen were at their best. *The Saturday Review* complained: ''Miss Terry is very charming, but she is not Juliet, and when real tragic passion is wanted, it is not forthcoming.'' James Wedmore was also critical and even such a devoted Lyceumite as Eleanor Marx felt let down:

> The most disappointing feature is the 'Juliet' — charming in the early scenes — comedy scenes so to say — Ellen Terry gets weaker and weaker as the tragic element appears till in the poison scene she collapses altogether.

Henry James reported to his American readers:

> Even though people are sadly bewildered by what they see and hear in it, they appear to recommend the performance to their friends. It has the advantage of that splendid scenic presentation which Mr Irving understands so well, and which converts the play from a splendid and delicate poem into a gorgeous and overweighted spectacle. Mr Irving does these things very handsomely; he is a most liberal and intelligent manager. It may, indeed, not be thought a proof of his intelligence that he himself should play the hero, or that he should entrust the girlish Juliet to the large, the long, the mature Miss Terry. Miss Terry has great charm; she is what the French call, in artistic parlance, a ''nature''; she is almost always interesting, and she is often a delightful presence: but she is not Juliet . . . . How little Mr Irving is Romeo, it is not worth while even to attempt to declare . . . much of the dialogue is incomprehensibly spoken . . . .

Left: Fanny Stirling was coaxed out of retirement in 1882 to re-create her most famous role — the Nurse to Ellen's Juliet. Photograph by Window & Grove. *Right:* Ellen played the role of Nurse herself at the Lyric, Hammersmith, in 1919. Photograph by Emil Otto Hoppé.

In his review for the magazine *The Theatre* of the 1882 Lyceum production of *Romeo and Juliet,* theatre critic Clement Scott remarked: ''The golden lattice, the sumptious surroundings, the foliage in the garden, the sky showing the pinks and oranges and purples of a sunrise, and at last, the golden sun itself, all are beautiful enough, but they are trying background for the centre figures.'' Amedée Forestieri documented the scene in a masterly piece of Victorian steel-engraving.

Left: Ellen as Beatrice in
Much Ado About Nothing, 1882.
Photograph by Window & Grove.

Johnston Forbes-Robertson's
painting of 'The Church Scene'
(Act IV, Scene i) from *Much
Ado About Nothing* featured
most of the principal actors at the
Lyceum in 1882. *From left to
right:* Miss Coleridge; Miss
Harwood; Ellen; James
Fernandez; Tom Mead; Jessie
Millward; Johnston Forbes-
Robertson; William Terriss; Henry
Irving; Charles Glenney; Miss
Mead; J. H. Allen; William
Haviland; Frank Tyars;
J. Robertson; Henry Howe. The
set was designed by W. L. Telbin.

Even Ellen herself was not satisfied:

> I am not going to say that Henry's Romeo was
> good . . . . I have read everything that had ever been
> written about [Juliet] before I had myself decided what
> she was. It was a dreadful mistake. That was the first
> thing wrong . . . lack of original impulse.

Irving's estranged wife, Florence, who lost no chance of mocking her husband's first nights, wrote in her diary: "Jolly failure — Irving awfully funny." Nevertheless, the production ran for 24 weeks to full houses until the end of the season.

When the company re-assembled after the summer break rehearsals began for *Much Ado About Nothing*. Of all Shakespeare's heroines it was generally agreed that Beatrice was the perfect role for Ellen. It is worth mentioning that Irving had one of his few almost wholly favourable critical receptions for his Benedick, though Ellen was not impressed: "Due to Henry's rather finicking deliberate method as Benedick, I could never put the right pace into my part." That notwithstanding, Beatrice was a great personal triumph for Ellen. Thereafter she often signed postcards: "A star danced and under that I was born." She was able to revive the whole play, or selected scenes, with no loss of conviction for the rest of her career.

Much Ado About Nothing opened on 11th October, 1882 and ran until the following June. On the last night, in the midst of one of his typically effusive and confused curtain speeches, Irving announced that the company would be away on a six-month tour of the provinces and America. Everyone went wild with excitement; Irving's fame was reaching its apogee.

On 11th October, 1883 Irving and Ellen sailed for New York on the *Britannic*; the rest of the company followed aboard the *City of Rome*. The press put to sea to greet them on their arrival, accompanied by a band playing 'Hail to the Chief'. In the newspapers the next day most of the attention was focussed on Irving but Ellen was not neglected. *The New York Herald* was generous in its coverage:

> A light veil half hid a pleasant face, a trifle thin but fairly radiant with animation. The grayish eyes were full of light, and the yellow hair crowned a pale, intelligent forehead. Miss Terry's figure is lithe, sinuous and handsome in its proportions. Every movement has a certain grace which the rough travelling dress she wore yesterday did not serve to hide. The actress is evidently a woman of extreme nervous sensibility, with an organisation so highly strung that in the words of a friend yesterday, "she always has her heart in her mouth." The muscles of her face respond to the slightest excitement, and her emotions are clearly reflected on it. The lady was in raptures over the warmth of her reception.

The New York Theatre was of course already long accustomed to seeing the best British actors but the Irving-Terry tour created unprecedented scenes. Joseph Hatton reported that: ". . . inclement

Right: Henry and Ellen as Mephistopheles and Margaret in W. G. Wills' *Faust*. Irving did not always use conventional stage make-up: for this role he painted his forehead and cheeks with blue watercolour paint. Ellen's pleated dress was one of several costumes from the play that Dame Nellie Melba copied for her appearances as Marguerite in Gounod's opera. This almost unique action photograph was taken on stage during the 1885 visit to the United States.

Right: Ellen as Viola disguised as Cesario in *Twelfth Night,* 1884. She wore this fairly convincing version of 19th-century Albanian male dress (embroidered with Turkish motifs to make it more dashing). Although this production was comparatively unsuccessful in London, where it suffered a calamitous first night, it proved to be the biggest hit of the subsequent American tour.

Far right: Henry Irving as Dr Primrose gazes tenderly at Ellen in the 1885 revival of *Olivia* by W. G. Wills.

weather, abnormal charges for seats, strong counter-attractions . . . made no difference.'' Ticket-scalpers had a field-day wherever they went.

The repertoire comprised: *The Bells, Charles I, Louis XI, The Merchant of Venice, The Lyons Mail* and *The Belle's Stratagem.* By April 1884 the company had visited a dozen cities (some twice); so successful was the tour that they arrived back in England with time only for a two-month season in London.

Irving decided on another Shakespeare revival: *Twelfth Night.* Unfortunately the production did not go down at all well, and Ellen managed to contract blood poisoning from an infected thumb during the first night and was forced to withdraw for the rest of the season. She was still not fit when the company's second tour of North America opened in Quebec on 30th September, 1884, but she was able to join them a couple of weeks later.

The strains and longueurs of this tour were particularly heavy and tedious but Ellen was as usual both a calming and cheering presence. Her son Teddy had been sent for and he made his stage debut in *Eugene Aram* in Chicago. The tour ended on a sad note for them both, with the news of Kelly's death on 17th April, 1885.

Back in London the company re-opened at the Lyceum with revivals of *Hamlet* and *Olivia.* By August Irving was full of plans for a brand new production — Goethe's *Faust*, adapted by W. G. Wills. He and Ellen set off on a working holiday to Germany to build up suitable background material, accompanied by Teddy and Edy, Hawes Craven (the Lyceum's resident designer), and Joseph and Alice Comyns Carr. Irving was clearly looking forward to creating a spectacular Mephistopheles, and so he did. The production opened on 19th December and had a phenomenal first run of 388 performances. Ellen's pathos as Margaret attracted as much acclaim as Irving's athleticism.

In September 1886 Ellen sent Teddy away to school and in October she heard that Godwin had died. At the Lyceum the following two years were a period of consolidation, with revivals in London, provincial tours, and a third visit to the United States.

The 1888 season opened on 14th April with *Faust* and then, on 23rd May, Ellen made her first appearance in a major production without Irving, in A. C. Calmour's *The Amber Heart.* It was a performance that attracted the eminent painter Edward Burne-Jones back to the theatre after a twenty-year absence. He wrote to the play's author: ''It is a most inspiring work to a painter — and Miss Terry's performance a revelation of loveliness.'' Ellen directed *The Amber Heart* herself (much to Irving's dismay) and was proud of her achievement of staging the whole production, using stock scenery and costumes, for only £15.

Right: Ellen in the dress designed for her by Mrs Comyns Carr for her role of Ellaline in *The Amber Heart,* 1887. *Below:* an Alfred Bryan caricature of Ellen as Ellaline.

MISS ELLALINE TERRY.

"See, see, our honour'd hostess!" John Singer Sargent made several sketches of Ellen as Lady Macbeth in 1888-89. This one (*above*) is a reworked version that was used in the souvenir programme for the Ellen Terry Jubilee in 1906.

Right: Lady Macbeth orders Macbeth to return the daggers to the dead Duncan's bedroom. Bernard Partridge manages to capture a certain ghostly eeriness and intensity in this drawing for the 1888 souvenir programme.

During the summer break Ellen had a holiday in Lucerne and then went with Irving to Scotland on a quest for 'local colour' for a revival of *Macbeth*. She was anxious to get away from the usual characterisation of Lady Macbeth as a fiendish woman driven by evil desire, opting instead for a more feline approach. *The Star* on 31st December was quick to appreciate her interpretation:

> The great fact about Miss Terry's Lady Macbeth is its sex. It is redolent, pungent with the *odeur de femme*. Look how she rushes into her husband's arms, clinging, kissing, coaxing, flattering, and even her taunts, when his resolution begins to wane, are sugared with a loving smile.

Lewis Carroll once again expressed popular opinion:

> Miss Ellen Terry was far better than I had thought possible. Irving was good. [George] Alexander as 'Macduff' was excellent. The scenery was superb.

Although Charles Cattermole had designed the other costumes for the production, Ellen's were made by Alice Comyns Carr. She had

Left: Sargent's celebrated oil painting of Ellen as Lady Macbeth shows her trying on a crown — an incident that occurs neither in Shakespeare's play nor in the Lyceum production. Ellen's costume, with its wide sleeves, became famous. *Right:* Lady Macbeth poised to receive her guests in another of her splendid 'Byzantine' dresses. It is obvious that Ellen could look grim if required.

HENRY IRVING AND ELLEN TERRY Recitals

Ellen and Henry capitalised on their success with *Macbeth* and toured a recital version in the summer of 1890. Note that Ellen is in costume while Irving is not. A caricature by Octopus.

devised a blood-red cloak for Lady Macbeth to put on after the murder of Duncan is discovered. Irving saw it at a dress rehearsal and advised Ellen to wear something more discreet. At the next rehearsal he turned up in the cloak himself.

Mrs Comyns Carr's undoubted *pièce de résistance* was a blue-green knitted wool and tinsel dress, which prompted Oscar Wilde to suggest that Lady Macbeth must have done her shopping in Byzantium. John Singer Sargent's portrait of Ellen wearing this costume attracted an immense amount of publicity and it is still the picture of her that is most frequently reproduced today. The American art historian Nina Auerbach suggests the reason for the portrait's durability:

> [It] represents, not Shakespeare's Lady Macbeth, but the apotheosis of Ellen Terry as she crowns herself with Shakespeare's character . . . . Ellen Terry into the diabolical Lady Macbeth, a composite creature who seems about to step out of her frame and force the viewer to kneel before her, crowns our icon of divine-demonic woman . . . a literary character embraces and fuels the self-glorification of the woman who portrays her.

It is possibly significant that Ellen chose this most advantageous time to reveal to the general public that she had a son old enough to play romantic heroes at the Lyceum. As a child Teddy had walked on in several productions but he made his official adult debut on 28th September, 1889. Under the name of Gordon Craig he appeared in *The Dead Heart*, a revised version of an old melodrama about the French

A delightfully informal family picture. Ellen with her children, Edy and Teddy, photographed by Frederick Hollyer in 1888.

Revolution. The play ran for 183 performances in spite of widely unfavourable reviews.

In *Ravenswood* (a stage version by Herman Merivale of Sir Walter Scott's novel *The Bride of Lammermoor*) Teddy was, according to *Moonshine*, "a nice young fellow, and very gifted like his Mama." That season mother and son appeared together in Charles Reade's *Nance Oldfield*, which Ellen described as "a great success, although my son and I did not know a word on the first night and had our parts written out and pinned all over the . . . stage."

Ellen as Lucy Ashton in Herman Merivale's *Ravenswood* (based on Sir Walter Scott's novel *The Bride of Lammermoor*) as seen by Bernard Partridge, 1890.

Ellen and her son Teddy appeared together in Charles Reade's *Nance Oldfield* in 1891. Moments later came the play's most popular piece of 'business'. Ellen collapsed onto the floor in a fit of giggles. Photograph by Window & Grove.

MISS ELLEN TERRY
as Queen Katherine

Seeking a tongue for tongueless shadow-land,
　Has Katherine's soul come back with power to quell
　A sister-soul incarnate and compel
It's fleshly voice to speak by Grief's command?
Or is it Katherine's self returns to stand
　As erst she stood defying Wolsey's spell—
　Returns with those wild wrongs she fain would tell
Which Memory bore to Eden's amaranth-strand?

Or is it thou, dear friend,—this Queen, whose face
　The salt of many tears hath scarred & stung?—
　Can it be thou, whose genius, ever young,
Lighting the body with the spirit's grace,
Is loved by England,—loved by all the race
　Round all the world enlinked by Shakspeare's
　　　　　　　　　　　　　tongue?

Theodore Watts

Ellen and Irving as Cordelia and Lear, 1892. The costumes were designed by the popular painter of historic subjects, Ford Madox Brown. Kate Terry-Gielgud recorded that, as Cordelia, Ellen "... looked like a girl of eighteen. She wears long draped frocks, one pale green, a lovely heavy white silk one and a grey, and has lank, real, (almost sandy) hair, drawn straight back from her face and tied at the nape of her neck. ... As she came on to the stage, the whole figure might have walked out of one of Burne-Jones's best pictures."

The poetic tribute to Ellen as Queen Katherine in *Henry VIII* is by Theodore Watts-Dunton, one of the lesser members of the Pre-Raphaelite circle. Bernard Partridge's drawing emphasises the costume's sleeves, which resembled those of Ellen's wedding dress.

By now Ellen was over forty and although she appeared in revivals of *Much Ado About Nothing, Olivia* and *Charles I*, it was becoming increasingly difficult to find suitable mature roles for her. One was found, which, like Lady Macbeth, had been played by Sarah Siddons — Queen Katherine in Shakespeare's *Henry VIII*. The production opened on 5th January, 1892 and was so spectacular that it ran for 203 performances. It was revived in the autumn while the company pressed on with preparations for *King Lear*. Irving was criticised for his characterisation of the King and critics complained more than usual of his inaudibility but Ellen as Cordelia was widely praised. She seemed to have found the secret of looking perpetually young on stage but Irving had to summon up all his strength at the end of one of Shakespeare's most arduous roles to carry her twelve-stone body in his arms without faltering.

Irving was undeterred by the failure of *King Lear* and immediately staged Tennyson's *Becket*, which opened on 6th February, 1893. It was Irving's last wholly successful production and the only one for which he received unanimous praise. Even the fastidious French critic Augustine Filon was impressed:

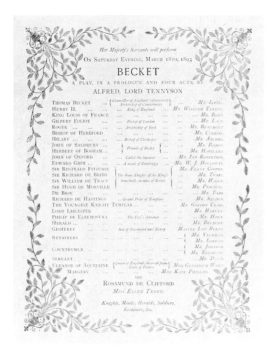

Windsor Castle was the setting for a Command Performance of Tennyson's *Becket* on 18th March, 1893. Reginald Cleaver sketched the scene below for *The Graphic*. Queen Victoria sits in the centre of the front row and on her left is her eldest son, Edward, Prince of Wales.

Right: Act III, Scene 3: Rosamund's Bower, designed by Hawes Craven. Becket (Henry Irving) prevents Eleanor of Aquitaine (Genevieve Ward) from stabbing Rosamund. Fitzurse (Frank Cooper) is the onlooker. *Below right:* Act IV, Scene 3: North Transept of Canterbury Cathedral, designed by W. L. Telbin. 'The assassins rush out, crying "King's Men!" Sir Hugh de Morville (Mr. Percival) follows slowly. Flashes of lightning through the Cathedral. Rosamund enters to kneel by Becket's body. CURTAIN.' This was the scene in which Irving made his last appearance on stage on the evening of his death in 1905. The Rosamund on that occasion was not Ellen, however, but Edith Wynne Matthison. Engravings by Andrew & Sleigh, from the souvenir programme.

Wilhelm del. '93

ROSAMUND

Those who saw Irving, mitred and crozier in hand totter under the blow, and fall upon the altar steps, whilst the chanting of the monks came in gusts from the church above — mingled with the cries of the people beating against the door, and the rumbling of the thunder shaking the great edifice to its foundations — experienced one of the strongest emotions any spectacle ever gave.

Most critics noticed that Ellen's part was extraneous to say the least but she remained as charming as ever. The production was so well received that the company was summoned to Windsor Castle to give a Royal Command Performance on 18th March. The Empress of Germany recalled the occasion:

> Irving acted well and with much dignity but his enunciation is not very distinct, especially when he gets excited. Ellen Terry as Rosamund was perfect, so graceful and full of feeling and so young-looking in her lovely light dress, quite wonderfully so for she is forty-six!

On 27th March, 1893 Teddy married for the first (and only) time and on 8th April his wife May Gibson gave birth to the first of Ellen's innumerable grandchildren.

The endorsement of products by entertainers is not a modern invention. Here Ellen promotes a rather curiously named hair preparation, wearing a hairdresser's striped cape. Among other products she advertised were Nixey's Blue (a whitener used when washing clothes); Cantrell and Cochrane's Belfast Ginger Ale; and Symington's soup. Photograph by Chancellors of Dublin.

Miss ELLEN TERRY, our Great Actress, writes:—
I have used "KOKO" for the Hair for years, and can assure my friends that it stops the Hair from falling out, promotes its growth, eradicates Dandriff, and is the most pleasant dressing imaginable.

At the Lyceum a steady routine of revivals continued and the winter of 1893-94 saw the company on another massive tour of North America. It was not until January 1895 that a new play entered the repertoire — *King Arthur* by Joseph Comyns Carr. The production was much influenced by Wagner's *Ring* cycle, which had been staged with great success at Covent Garden in June 1892, and it appealed to the Victorian passion for the romanticism of the Arthurian legend. William Archer liked the pageantry but was not too sure about Ellen's performance. In *The Theatrical World* of 1895 he wrote:

> The best written passage in the play . . . is the declaration between Lancelot and Guinevere. If Miss Ellen Terry had been a tragic and passionate instead of an idyllic and fascinating actress this would have been a thrilling moment . . .

Ironically, it was this same scene that Shaw picked upon when he wrote to Archer on 22nd February, 1901:

> Now the whole history of the Lyceum is the history of Herodifying Shakespeare — getting the brains and realism out and the Belsize Park suburban Jewish glamour in. Ellen Terry and Forbes-Robertson as Guinevere and Lancelot . . . was Lyceum ritual *in excelsis*.

In 1896 Irving mounted a new production of *Cymbeline*, with Ellen as Imogen. Shaw had a field-day criticising both the production and the play in a famous review entitled 'Blaming the Bard', but Henry James had mellowed:

> Miss Terry . . . grows younger and younger, and in her beautiful melancholy boy's dress shows admirably that the more chance she has for freedom of motion the more easily she surmounts its danger.

The year ended unhappily for both Irving and Ellen. Severe eye trouble, probably caused by the Lyceum's gas lights, forced Ellen to withdraw over the Christmas period, and Irving slipped and injured his knee on his way home from the theatre on the opening night of *Richard III*. With both stars out of action, the Lyceum went dark for the whole of January 1897.

For the following twelve months Irving seemed dogged by ill-fortune. The Lyceum's store of scenery was burnt, and the actor William Terriss, who had been with the company in the 1880's, was murdered. Irving put on a less than satisfactory play by his son Laurence — *Peter the Great* — and there was one complete disaster: *The Medicine Man* by Robert Hitchen and H. D. Traill, which marked Ellen and Irving's first appearance together in modern dress.

Ellen bought Tower Cottage, Winchelsea from Mr. and Mrs. Comyns Carr in 1895.

Ellen 'going a-maying' as Guinevere in Act II of *King Arthur* by Joseph Comyns Carr, 1895. *Above left:* A prosaic Window & Grove photograph shows the 'reality'. *Above right:* Bernard Partridge provides a 'documentary' illustration. *Right:* Pamela Colman Smith develops the image romantically.

In her forty-ninth year, when she played Imogen, Ellen managed to look remarkably young (*left*). She later wrote a melodramatic inscription on her own copy of this photograph by Window & Grove: "Think of me like this. Goodbye everybody at the Farm, 192–." (The last digit was left blank.) *Right:* As Volumnia, in the 1901 production of *Coriolanus*, Ellen is swathed in a toga-like creation made from one of her old dresses embellished with embroidery.

In June 1897 Bram Stoker, Irving's business manager, emerged as a public figure in his own right when his horror novel *Dracula* was published. It is now generally believed that Stoker based his character of Count Dracula on Irving himself:

> His face was a strong — very strong — aquiline, with high bridge of the thin nose, and peculiarly arched nostrils, with lofty domed forehead, and hair growing scantily round the temples, but profusely elsewhere. His eyebrows were very massive, almost meeting over the nose, and with bushy hair that seems to curl in its own profusion.

Stoker's pen-portrait of a dominating, yet always ailing, figure, who could live only by sucking blood from others and who came to life only at night, might have seemed familiar to many a long-suffering Lyceum employee.

Similarly, the heroines of Stoker's stories must have appeared to bear more than a passing resemblance to Ellen who, according to W. Graham Robertson, ". . . was a daughter of the night, happy in its shadow and mystery and loving the moon with a strange ecstasy which I have never met with in another."

During the autumn of 1898 Ellen and Irving undertook separate tours of the provinces. The following spring Irving relinquished the Lyceum's lease. They did tour together in the autumn of 1899 but by then the prospect of a permanent split in their partnership was common public knowledge.

The passing of the years was at last admitted when Ellen appeared as Volumnia to Irving's Coriolanus in April 1901. Later that year they embarked on their seventh and final tour of America together.

SIR HENRY IRVING AND MISS ELLEN TERRY ON ONE OF THEIR LAST PROVINCIAL TOURS.

The Lyceum company on tour in Yorkshire in 1900. Cartoon by Pamela Colman Smith.

Ellen and Henry. Drawing from the *Madame Sans-Gêne* souvenir programme.

6. Ellen and Henry

Ellen Terry and Henry Irving maintained a professional relationship for almost thirty years. It is not surprising, therefore, that there has been endless speculation about their relationship offstage. Ellen's daughter Edy claimed that the couple were lovers in the fullest sense while her son Teddy always adamantly denied this although he confirmed that Ellen and Irving often continued to act out their roles offstage. Margaret Webster, the daughter of Ben Webster and Dame May Whitty, speculated on the mystery and emphasised that it was not impertinent to do so since it was all part of the Irving-Terry phenomenon:

> Society took it for granted; but then society regarded Ellen Terry as a 'fallen woman', though it thought her more sinned against than sinning, and loved and forgave her . . . . By the time my parents joined the Lyceum company, and during the years when they grew to know Ellen Terry well, the earlier ardours had cooled. But they would both have been greatly surprised by the notion that there had never been more between her and Irving than good comradeship and professional association.

Offstage Ellen and Henry were undoubtedly close friends and often took holidays together. In 1885 Irving bought a country house with an enormous garden at Brook Green, then still a rural part of Hammersmith. He had lots of alterations made to the house and furnished it beautifully but lived there himself infrequently. If he had envisaged the house as a suitable home for himself, Ellen and her children, there were two very good reasons why Ellen would have rejected any idea of marriage. Firstly, Irving had established for himself, by the mid-1880's, a convivially Bohemian life-style, which Ellen did not really share. Secondly, and more importantly, however, was the problem of Irving's estranged wife Florence, who could have wrecked their careers if asked to involve herself in a public divorce scandal.

It had not escaped the attention of audiences and critics that Irving seemed to give himself at least one speech in each play where he could pour out his heart to Ellen on stage. Ellen did not appear every night at the Lyceum, of course, and while she was living in the country she and Irving corresponded constantly. Unfortunately nearly all of their letters have been destroyed. In one letter from Irving, however, he does refer to Ellen as "my own dear wife, as long as I live."

Most recent biographers have stated quite bluntly that Ellen and Irving were definitely lovers, explaining that it is quite natural for families (especially sons) to try and conceal the truth from the world. The fact remains, however, that there is no definite proof one way or the other. As Dame May Whitty crisply declared: "Though of course no-one was actually under the bed!" But perhaps the last word should be given to Lady Duff Gordon, who was a frequent visitor to Ellen's house in Longridge Road:

> Henry Irving used to drift in and out at all hours, looking very eccentric sometimes. She [Ellen] understood him perfectly and always knew how to manage him. Once or twice I saw him in a towering rage, working himself up to fever heat over something that had happened at the theatre, but she could calm him in a moment. It always struck me that their association was one of closest friendship rather than love. She told me the same herself.
>
> "People always say that Henry is my lover of course. He isn't. As a matter of fact he never sees further than my head. He does not even know I have a body."

1897: the year of the pince-nez. *Left:* Ellen in a picturesque tea-gown from Liberty's. *Right:* Sir Henry receiving the honorary degree of Doctor of Letters from Cambridge University.

Ellen and Henry as Imogen and Iachimo in the Lyceum production of *Cymbeline.* The drawing by S. Begg appeared in *The Illustrated London News* on 23rd May, 1896.

7. Craig, Shaw and a Jubilee

HERBERT BEERBOHM TREE, a successful actor during the late 1870's and early 1880's, established himself as an actor-manager at the Haymarket from 1887-96 and then at the re-built Her Majesty's Theatre from 1897. He represented a serious challenge to Irving, with a repertoire of modern plays as well as spectacular Shakespearean revivals.

It is perhaps significant that Tree could attract the financial backing to reconstruct Her Majesty's Theatre to the highest safety standards required by the London authorities whereas Irving was unable to do the same at the increasingly shabby Lyceum. In fact, so parlous had Irving's affairs become that in 1899 he was declared bankrupt. After that, the Lyceum was run by a syndicate and Irving lost his autonomy. Eventually the building was found to be in such a poor condition that the London County Council threatened to close it down unless major repairs were carried out.

There were so many alterations stipulated and the costs were so high that the directors of the Lyceum decided to demolish and re-build the entire structure from the front to the back wall of the stage area. The new building, designed by Bertie Crewe, opened as a variety theatre in 1904, thus ending a golden era in theatre history.

Ellen did appear in a hastily arranged season at the old Lyceum in the summer of 1902 but she was beginning to make other arrangements. She had already played Katherine in Shakespeare's *Henry VIII* for F. R. Benson at the Memorial Theatre in Stratford-upon-Avon and she soon received an invitation from Beerbohm Tree, who wanted her for *The Merry Wives of Windsor*.

The actor Oscar Asche described how Ellen came to be chosen:

> Tree decided to revive *Merry Wives*, with Lily Hanbury and Mrs Tree as the two wives and Lily Brayton as Anne Page. But dear Lily Hanbury had a nervous breakdown and had to resign. "What shall we do now Asche?" said Tree . . . . Quite jokingly I suggested Ellen Terry and Madge Kendal. He looked at me: "Yes! Yes!".

A version in oils of the pastel portrait of Ellen at Smallhythe by W. Graham Robertson, 1891. It was presented by Edy Craig to the Ellen Terry National Home for the Blind in 1925 and donated to the Bristol University Theatre Collection after the Home's closure in 1984.

Anyhow, after the show that night Tree motored to Mrs Kendal's house in Portland Place. She consented to play if she had choice of parts. She chose Mistress Ford. Then Tree motored to Winchelsea, where Ellen Terry had a house. Yes, she would play, but must play Mistress Page. So all was clear sailing . . . . I produced it for Tree and it played to sensational business, Ellen Terry making a personal triumph.

The Merry Wives of Windsor opened at Her Majesty's on 10th June, 1902 and was indeed a personal triumph for Ellen. The production ran for 156 performances. The critic Max Beerbohm (Tree's half-brother) analysed the success and came to the conclusion that this was due to:

> . . . the sensational juxtaposition of Mrs Kendal and Miss Ellen Terry as Mistress Ford and Mistress Page. A greater contrast could hardly be conceived. On the one hand Miss Terry, with her exuberant, sun-bright charm, her spontaneous jollity and, above all, her long training in Shakespearean plays; on the other hand, Mrs Kendal, with her neat, trim, delightfully prosaic method, her quick, quiet, unadorned realism. It is needless to say which of these two in a play of this kind plays the other off the stage.

Even though she appeared under-rehearsed on the first night Ellen could do no wrong; the critic on *The Standard* was captivated:

> It did not matter at all that Ellen Terry did not know her 'words', that she read from printed pages scattered for her about the stage, and that the company prompted her. The audience crooned with pleasure, and filled up all the blanks.

Notwithstanding her success, Irving still insisted that Ellen carry out her obligations to him as well, and so she played in matinées of *Charles I* and *The Merchant of Venice*.

In the spring of 1903 Irving presented a new play, *Dante*, adapted from the French by his son Laurence, at Drury Lane. The role of Beatrice was an obvious one for Ellen but by this time she was no longer a member of the company. She did join Irving for an all-star Actors' Benevolent Fund matinée of *The Merchant of Venice* on 14th July, 1903, however. It was to prove their very last performance together.

In the autumn Irving left for his last tour of the United States. He wrote to the American critic William Winter:

> It will be strange and somewhat sad without Nell . . . . Poor dear, she has been absolutely under the influence

Ellen (*left*) as Mistress Page and Madge Kendal as Mistress Ford with Herbert Beerbohm Tree as Falstaff in *The Merry Wives of Windsor*, Act II, Scene iii. Painting by the Hon. John Collier.

and spell of her two children — who have launched her on a sea of troubles.

Edy and Teddy had both acted on stage, at the Lyceum and elsewhere, but both gradually developed an interest in design. With a subsidy from Ellen, Edy eventually established herself as a costumier. The relationship between mother and daughter had never been cosy and things became very difficult when Edy met Christabel Marshall, with whom she was to form a life-long partnership.

Christabel had seen Edy in a play in Bristol and immediately fell in love. They corresponded regularly and set up house together in 1899 when Christabel was working as a secretary to Lady Randolph Churchill. Ellen eventually accepted the relationship and indeed came to depend on the couple for advice and support. When she settled into her last home, at Smallhythe, she bought them the nearby Priest's House.

Edy and Christabel (or Christopher St John as she later became, having changed her name by deed poll) were active feminists and together they formed the Pioneer Players in 1911, with Edy as principal designer and director.

Although Ellen and Edy often disagreed over men, there was one they both adored — Teddy — whom they had spoiled from infancy onwards. After leaving the Lyceum company in 1897 Teddy, now known as [Edward] Gordon Craig, had gained a considerable reputation as an illustrator and writer. He had stopped acting altogether by the turn of the century and in 1901 and 1902 presented productions of Henry Purcell's *Dido and Aeneas* and Laurence Housman's *Bethlehem*, with amateur casts and striking scenery of his own design.

By 1903 Craig had persuaded Ellen to finance his first professional production. She leased the Imperial Theatre from Lillie Langtry and appeared under Craig's direction in Ibsen's only costume play, *The Vikings*. Ellen and Craig had read the play aloud on Christmas day and to her it seemed:

> . . . tremendous. Not in my most wildly optimistic moments did I think Hjordis [sic] . . . a primitive, fighting, free, open-air person — suited to me, but I saw a way of playing her more brilliantly and less weightily than the text suggested, and anyhow I was not thinking so much of the play for me as for my son.

With three strong-willed members of the family working together (Edy made the costumes), there was bound to be friction. The part of Hiordis was another virago but one who could not, unfortunately, be 'humanised' without upsetting the play completely. Many critics noticed this — and Ellen's nervousness on the first night — but most were concerned with Craig's settings and in particular his gloomy, Lyceum-like lighting effects.

W. B. Yeats was among those present on the first night. He wrote to Lady Gregory:

> I saw *Vikings* last night. I liked Ellen Terry in it and liked moments of the play altogether and it all interested me. Craig's scenery is amazing but rather distracts one's thoughts from the words . . . . I suggested that the fortunes of the theatre might be retrieved (house was half empty) by their imitating *The Times* and having a prize competition. So many hundreds for anybody who could hear three lines together and £5 a piece for words heard anywhere . . . . Of course, however, the play is better worth seeing than anything else that has been

Left: Amedée Forestieri's impression of Act II of *The Vikings* by Ibsen does less than justice to Edward Gordon Craig's revolutionary designs for the 1903 production at the Imperial Theatre. *From left to right:* Conway Tearle (Torolf); Holman Clarke (Ornulf); Ellen (Hiordis); Hutin Britton (Dagny); Oscar Asche (Sigurd).

Right: Photographer Leonard Craske took Ellen onto the beach at Swansea in her costume as Kniertje in *The Good Hope* by Dutch dramatist Herman Heijermans (1904) and so provided a very early example of the theatrical publicity shot taken 'on location'.

here this long while and for this reason it is failing. Ellen Terry when I saw her for a moment after it was over said: ''Well it is a fine play to have made a failure with.'' She added that everybody there had got a good living wage out of it and so it did not matter — everybody but she herself who would get nothing. She impresses me a good deal by her vitality and a kind of joyousness.

In 1904 G. F. Watts died and Craig left England to live in Paris. Ellen appeared in a modern 'realistic' play — *The Good Hope* by the Dutch dramatist Herman Heijermans. She and Edy toured it successfully before returning in April 1905 to London where Ellen was to play under Charles Frohman's management in J. M. Barrie's *Alice Sit-By-The-Fire*. But fashions were changing, as Max Beerbohm perceived:

It seems appropriate that Miss Ellen Terry should be in a Barrie play. For her, among actresses, the public has the same sort of affection as it had for Mr Barrie among dramatists. And her genius, like his, is ever childish and irresponsible. But, while his genius is a delicate and

modern one, hers is very boisterous, and seems to belong rather to 'the spacious days' than to ours . . . . The part which Miss Terry plays here is the part of Mrs Gray, the mother of Amy and of the baby; and Mrs Gray is an impulsive and exuberant woman. But Miss Terry is really too exuberant, too impulsive. The play is not big enough for her. Like Mrs Gray with the baby, she all but smothers it in the fervour of her embrace. One longs for Shakespeare, who, alone among dramatists, can stand up to her and one wishes the theatre itself were bigger — better proportioned to the wildly ample sweep of her method.

Irving was taken seriously ill while on tour in February 1905 but he gradually recovered and insisted on touring again in the autumn with two of his most strenuous productions: *The Bells* and *Becket*. On 13th October he appeared as Becket in Bradford and died within minutes of leaving the theatre — in the entrance hall of the Midland Hotel.

Following representations from a distinguished group of 'humble petitioners', Irving was buried in Westminster Abbey. Ellen was the only woman in the funeral procession and her description of the event is one of her most vivid pieces of writing:

How terribly I missed that face at Henry's own funeral: I kept on expecting to see it, for indeed it seemed to me that he was directing the whole most moving and impressive ceremony. I could almost hear him saying ''Get on! get on!'' in the part of the service that dragged. When the sun — such a splendid, tawny sun — burst across the solemn misty grey of the Abbey, at the very moment when the coffin, under its superb pall of laurel leaves, was carried up the choir, I felt that it was an effect which he would have loved.

It was probably only after Irving's death that Ellen felt free to commit herself to the play that George Bernard Shaw had written specially for her: *Captain Brassbound's Conversion*. (She had played only in the copyright performance given in Liverpool in 1898.)

Shaw had sent the first of his many letters to Ellen in 1892 and they had amused themselves with a flamboyant 'paper courtship' since 1896. Shaw had publicly criticised Irving for failing to recognise the New Drama and had even gone so far as to write *Man of Destiny* with him and Ellen in mind. By the time Ellen was ready to accept the role of Lady Cicely Waynflete in *Captain Brassbound's Conversion* in 1906 Shaw was married and Ellen too was soon to find a new husband, as Shaw himself recalled:

Ellen as Alice in *Alice Sit-By-The-Fire* by J. M. Barrie, 1905. *Above:* with Dora Hole as Nurse and C. Aubrey Smith as Colonel Gray. *Right:* A. E. Matthews played the romantic lead.

The door opened, and a young American actor, James Carew . . . came in. ''Who is that?'' said Ellen, looking at him with quick interest. ''That's the American captain,'' I answered. Without an instant's hesitation she sailed across the room; put Mr Carew in her pocket (so to speak); and married him.

Ellen sent Teddy a postcard from Niagara Falls:

> 1 March 1907. Dear Duck — This is Jim and me — we are married — long ago — You don't mind much, do you? We had to keep it secret until we left off acting before American audiences — not caring to be a kind of circus. James Carew is an American — only 32 and a half but as old as the hills. I love him dearly. I neglect no responsibilities.

By this time Ellen had been an actress for fifty years and so to commemorate her jubilee in 1906 a spectacular benefit matinée was mounted for her at the Theatre Royal, Drury Lane.

The matinée was an enormous success and £6,000 was raised with a further £3,000 collected from public donations. Crowds were already gathering outside the theatre the day before; the producer and director Basil Dean witnessed the excitement:

> It must have been one of the earliest instances of an all-night theatre queue. My brother and I were determined to get good seats in the pit (at ten shillings each). We arrived at nine o'clock in the evening, to find some thirty or forty people there before us. By midnight news of the queue had drawn the town. The street leading to the stage door was crowded with playgoers returning home, including the 'haut monde' from the Grand Opera Season, with market idlers and people of every sort, all come to gape and see the fun.
>
> We stormed into the pit about noon only to find it had been reduced to half its size to make room for additional stalls. Many of those who had waited confidently all night found themselves jammed tightly into standing rows at the back. Late-comers were sent away in hundreds. There were angry shouts and cries against the management. Some of the rougher elements began to break up the seating. My brother and I had secured places in the centre of the second row, but we were not sure that we were going to be allowed to stay there. Appeals from the attendants and assistant managers were drowned in the Hubbub.

Ellen as Elizabeth of York and James Carew as Henry in *Henry of Lancaster* by Gladys B. Ungar, 1908.

In 1906 a benefit matinée was presented at the Drury Lane Theatre to celebrate Ellen's jubilee of fifty years as a professional actress.

Left: A popular version of the programme was reproduced on paper serviettes and sold on the streets to commemorate the event. A vignette of Ellen in her famous 'toreador' hat is flanked by portraits of Edward VII and Queen Alexandra. Altogether 400 people took part although the programme was not presented in the order listed.

Above: 'A cast of Terrys at Ellen Terry's Benefit. Three Fair and Clever Sisters and Their Kinsfolk in Much Ado About Nothing.' So ran the caption when *The Sketch* reproduced this Dover Street Studios photograph in its issue of 20th June. Kate (centre) is flanked by Marion (left) and Ellen (right). Brother Fred is on the extreme right. The set and costumes used were those that Edward Gordon Craig had designed for his 1903 production of *Much Ado About Nothing*.

Eventually, Arthur Collins had to be sent for. He came stalking down the centre aisle in the stalls in top hat and frock-coat, waving his arms and appealing for quiet. When the din subsided, he pointed out that the pit had been reduced in size (''No pit left, guv'nor'') in order to make as much money as possible for 'our beloved Ellen'. (''Hear, hear! Boo! Quite right! Boo! Bet she knows nothing about it. Three cheers for our Ellen!'') Eventually order was restored.

In 1908 Ellen published her autobiography, *The Story of my Life*. It was generally well received although L. Carson found that:

> Her tone respecting several of her professional colleagues was less amiable than one would fain have hoped from this charming and distinguished actress.

Ellen had been helped by Christopher St John in producing the book but she was a fluent writer with a natural talent for the telling phrase, and the result was a most entertaining and informative account of her theatrical life.

A family gathering at Smallhythe in 1906. *From left to right:* Elena Meo (Teddy and Rosie's mother); Edward 'Teddy' Craig (Ellen's grandson); Ellen; Edward Gordon Craig; Rosemary 'Rosie' Craig (Ellen's granddaughter).

1912

M^{ISS} ELLEN TERRY

RECITAL

PROGRAMME
THREEPENCE.

By arrangement with the
QUINLAN INTERNATIONAL
MUSICAL AGENCY,
318 Regent Street, London, W.

8. The Final Years

CHRISTOPHER ST JOHN published anonymously a novel entitled *Hungerheart: The Story of a Soul* in 1915. This was a thinly disguised autobiography in which she enshrined her love for Edy (as Sally) and her admiration for Ellen (as Louise Canning) and Irving (as Mark Washington). Ellen's latest husband, James Carew, however, was not admired and Chris and Edy were allegedly delighted when the couple were judicially separated after just two years of marriage.

After the separation Ellen embarked on a flurry of activity, largely organised by Chris and Edy, who were still dependent on her to subsidise their theatrical ventures.

Since the 1890's, however, Ellen's health had been declining. In 1912 she suffered a complete breakdown and spent several months in a nursing home run by a Miss Pollock. Typically she came up with a vivid phrase of her own to describe her condition: 'ditheration of the brain'.

Ellen played the Mother in a propaganda film called *Invasion of Britain*, which was made during the First World War. José Collins played the Daughter-in-law. The film, which was never released as it was not completed until the War was almost over, is now lost.

Left: "Miss Ellen Terry will give a Shakespearean recital with illustrative acting on some of the heroines from Shakespeare's plays." During her 1912 January tour Ellen appeared in twelve towns in the north of England and East Anglia in 24 days, concluding with a 'special flying matinée' in Brighton. Photograph taken in Alexander Ridley's studio at Tenterden.

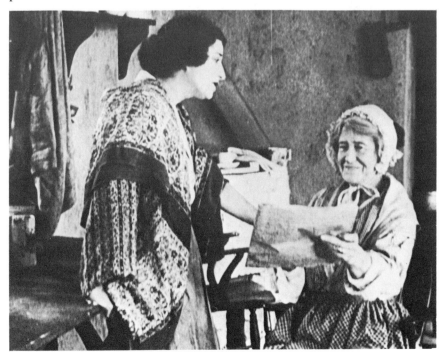

J. M. Barrie (seated at the table) rehearsing his 'All Star Cast' on the roof of Wyndham's Theatre for a charity performance of *The Admirable Crichton* at the London Coliseum on 9th June, 1916.

1. George Bernard Shaw. 2. Charles Hawtry. 3. Arthur Bourchier. 4. George Grossmith. 5. Dennis Eadie. 6. Sydney Valentine. 7. Leslie Henson. 8. Sir George Alexander. 9. Lady Wyndham (Miss Mary Moore). 10 Miss Dorothy Minto. 11. Ben Webster. 12. Edmund Gwenn. 13. Miss Claire Greet. 14. Miss Lillian Braithwaite. 15. Miss May Whitty. 16. Eric Lewis. 17. John Drinkwater. 18. Miss Polly Emery. 19. Miss Hilda Trevelyan. 20. Miss Madge Titheradge. 21. Gerald du Maurier. 22. Sir J. M. Barrie. 23. Miss Gladys Cooper. 24. Miss Nina Boucicault. 25. Sir Johnston Forbes-Robertson. 26. Lady Forbes-Robertson. 27. Miss Vesta Tilley. 28. Miss Ellen Terry. 29. Miss Lillah McCarthy. 30. Miss Compton. 31. Miss Lily Elsie. Photograph by W. Graham Robertson.

She recovered sufficiently to embark on a series of lecture tours and to make personal appearances. The lectures consisted of recitations of individual speeches from Shakespeare with her own commentaries, suitably written up by Chris. She was thus able to give her audiences something of the magic for which she had become legendary without the strain of a full-scale performance.

But increasingly she relied on her 'Old Dear' image. The actor A. E. Matthews had observed her technique at close hand when he appeared with her in *Alice Sit-By-The-Fire* in 1905:

> Each night she would give a different rendering of her part, handling it according to the inspiration she got from the particular audience. As audiences varied so did her performances . . . . She always carried several handbags hanging on her arms; one we knew contained lunch but the purpose of the extra three or four puzzled

Ellen with Gladys Cooper in *The Bohemian Girl*, a silent film made in 1922.

us all. At the first rehearsal it was understandable that Miss Terry should be late for her entrance . . . she appeared, smiled graciously and promptly dropped her handbags — all four of them. Of course, we all rushed forward in a bunch to pick them up . . . one by one the bags were passed to Miss Terry who calmly threaded them on her arm, thanked us with a smile and then spoke her opening speech just as if nothing had happened. When this bag-dropping business occurred at every rehearsal we began to suspect it was not quite accidental . . . . The real purpose of the bag-dropping eluded us until the opening night. Then on her cue, there occurred that uncomfortable pause — hoarse whisperings at the sides growing to calls for 'Miss Terry' that even the audience could hear. The whole house began to dread that Ellen Terry was too ill to

Ellen herself inscribed this sketch by Marguerite Steen: 'E.T. & her Bag!' She appeared at the Everyman Theatre, Hampstead in December, 1920, to speak the Prologue to a Nativity Play.

Still working, Ellen arrives to lay the foundation stone of the Playhouse, Walton-on-Thames in 1925. This was one of the many public appearances she made during the 1920's which served to keep the memory of her personality alive long after she had ceased to act regularly on stage.

ELLEN TERRY.

XMAS 1920.
Hampstead
Stage door.
Everyman Theatre.

E.T. & her Bag!

appear. When she at last floated onto the stage their relief gave greater warmth to the tumultuous applause . . . . Overcome by this ovation, she waited for the clapping to cease, then dropping her arms with a graceful gesture, down went the cluster of bags. The famous and much loved 'Terry charm' merited, and demanded, a further round of applause, as she graciously received her handbags one by one. When they were once again safely on her arms, the whole audience was hers alone.

In January 1925 Ellen was awarded the D.B.E. (Dame of the British Empire), an honour that many of her admirers felt she should have received in 1921 when Genevieve Ward became the first British actress to be created a Dame.

Ellen's last stage appearance was as a ghost in Walter de la Mare's *Crossings* in November, 1925. Thereafter she became frailer but made some public appearances and visited friends whenever possible. By the beginning of 1928, however, she seemed to be, as W. Graham Robertson put it: ". . . drifting away into a vague world where nothing is real and people bear no names."

Ellen Terry finally passed away in a bedroom made up for her on the ground floor of her farmhouse at Smallhythe at 8.30 on the morning of 21st July, 1928.

'Portia hurrying for the train'.
A drawing by Pamela Colman
Smith, from the 1890's.

A Note on Sources

GENERAL

Most of Ellen Terry's own words are taken from *The Story of My Life* (Hutchinson 1908). This was extensively revised (with some curious excisions) and re-issued as *Ellen Terry's Memoirs* (Gollanz 1933). Edy Craig and Christopher St John contributed a preface, notes and additional biographical chapters. Ellen's plain-spokenness and perceptive comments make this one of the very best of all theatre autobiographies.

The principal repository of Ellen Terry memorabilia and associated papers is the Ellen Terry Memorial Museum, Smallhythe Place, Smallhythe, Tenterden, Kent TN30 7NG (telephone 05806 2334). The house, Ellen's final home, was presented to the National Trust by Edy Craig in 1939. It is open to the public from April to October (every day except Tuesdays and Fridays). Advance arrangements should be made for large parties or visits outside the normal opening hours.

Additional Ellen Terry documents are to be found at: Bristol Record Office; Hillingdon Public Libraries Local Collection; Theatre Museum, London; Shakespeare Centre Library, Stratford-upon-Avon. Harvester Microfilm of Brighton publish the Stratford holdings on microfiche, together with a full descriptive catalogue in 'Britain's Literary Heritage: Actors and Managers of the English and American Theatre, Series One: *The Papers of Henry Irving and Ellen Terry*' (1987).

Roger Manvell's *Ellen Terry* (Heinemann 1968) and Tom Prideaux's *Love or Nothing* (Scribner's Sons 1975) are based on sound research from mainly secondary sources. Both are poorly illustrated, though not as badly as Nina Auerbach's *Ellen Terry* (J. M. Dent 1987), which does, however, incorporate a mass of new research into Ellen's voluminous correspondence; this is a feminist view of Ellen's life and career, and her relationship with Edy looms large. The mother/daughter relationship is the whole topic of Joy Melville's smoothly written and well illustrated (entirely from the Smallhythe archive) *Ellen & Edy* (Pandora Books 1987).

In *A Pride of Terrys* (Longmans 1962) Marguerite Steen presents Ellen in the context of the ramifications of her amazing family. Michael Booth analyses her 'pictorial' archetype in his study of her in *Bernhardt, Terry, Duse* (Cambridge University Press 1988).

Smallhythe Place, Tenterden, c.1905.

INTRODUCTION

Winston Churchill's typically succinct phrase comes from a tribute to Ellen Terry published in *The Times* (19th June 1906).

Sarah Bernhardt recorded her impressions of her contemporary in *Memories of My Life* (1907).

George Bernard Shaw discussed Ellen in an essay on her sister Kate, reprinted in *Dramatic Opinions, Volume 2* (Constable 1913).

Alfred Sutro's story is in *Celebrities Are Simple Souls* (Duckworth 1933).

Sir Frank Benson's recollection is one of *My Memoirs* (Benn 1930).

Henry James's dramatic reviews were collected as *The Scenic Art* (Rupert Hart-Davis 1949).

W. Graham Robertson's graphic description of Ellen's stage dresses is in *Time Was* (Hamilton 1931).

Edith Evans recalled working with Ellen in her TV interview with Hal Burton reprinted in *Great Acting* (BBC 1967).

The quotation from Charles Reade's notebook was first used in Malcolm Elwin's *Charles Reade* (Cape 1931).

Lady Cynthia Asquith's account of meeting Ellen is recorded in her *Diaries 1915-1918* (Hutchinson 1968).

Florence Hardy included her husband's note in *The life of Thomas Hardy* (Macmillan 1962).

THE EARLY YEARS

The Diaries of Lewis Carroll were edited by Roger Lancelyn Green in two volumes (Cassell 1953).

E. L. Blanchard's *Life and Reminiscences* were edited by Clement Scott and Cecil Howard (Hutchinson 1891).

G. F. WATTS

The main source for biographical information on George Frederick Watts is *England's Michaelangelo* by Wilfred Blunt (Hamilton 1975).

The Ellen-Watts marriage was the subject of *Sweet Lost Years* (Collins 1966), a romantic historical novel by Laura Conway.

Henry Silver's diary is unpublished.

Letters from W. Graham Robertson were edited by the recipient, Kerrison Preston (Hamilton 1953).

A. M. W. Stirling's account of the Ellen-Watts relationship is in *Life's Little Day* (Butterworth 1924).

H. Allingham and D. Radford edited *The Diary of William Allingham* (Macmillan 1907).

Lewis Carroll's comments are from his *Diaries*.

E. W. GODWIN

Although he was one of the key figures in the development of Victorian architecture and design, Godwin has received surprisingly little serious coverage. Principal sources include: Dudley Harbron's *The Conscious Stone* (Latimer House 1949); H. Montgomery Hyde's essay on 'Oscar Wilde and His Architect' in *Edwardian Architecture and Its origins*; 'An Aesthetic Theatre' in *Resistible Theatres* (Elek 1972); Gordon Craig's *Index to the Story of My Days* (Hulton Press 1957); and Edward Craig's *Gordon Craig* (Gollanz 1968).

The quotation from W. Graham Robertson is taken from a letter to Kerrison Preston.

RETURN TO THE STAGE

Johnston Forbes-Robertson's description of his first meeting with Ellen comes from *A Player Under Three Reigns* (Fisher Unwin 1925).

Lewis Carroll's notes are from his *Diaries*.

Henry James's reviews are published in *The Scenic Art*.

Clement Scott's analysis of Olivia is from *Ellen Terry* (Stokes 1900).

Edgar Pemberton's account of the Olivia craze is from *Ellen Terry and Her Sisters* (C. Arthur Pearson 1902).

William Poel's criticism is quoted by Robert Speaight in *William Poel and the Elizabethan Revival* (Heinemann 1954).

Dutton Cook's review is from *Nights at the Play* (Chatto & Windus 1883).

IRVING AND THE LYCEUM

Irving was even more heavily documented by his contemporaries than Ellen. Austin Brereton's massive *Life of Henry Irving* (Longmans 1908) and Bram Stoker's *Personal Reminiscences of Henry Irving* (Heinemann 1907) are still fascinating and essential.

Although Madeleine Bingham tried to find some new angles for her *Henry Irving* (Allen & Unwin 1978) it seems superficial when compared with Laurence Irving's magisterially thorough and yet eminently readable *Henry Irving* (Faber 1951). The model theatrical biography, it was reprinted in 1989. From it come John Ruskin's letter and Florence Irving's typical reaction to her husband's acting.

Alan Hughes' *Henry Irving, Shakespearean* (Cambridge University Press 1981) was among the first scholarly treatments of his career.

Lewis Carroll's reminiscences are from his *Diaries*.

William Archer included his interview with Henry Howe in *Masks or Faces?* (Longmans 1888).

Max Beerbohm's reviews are from *Around Theatres* (Rupert Hart-Davis 1953).

Henry Labouchaire's comments on *The Cup* appeared in *The Truth* on 13th January, 1881.

Oscar Wilde's first-night note is from *The Letters of Oscar Wilde* (Rupert Hart-Davis 1962).

Eleanor Marx's diary entry is in Chushichi Tsuzuki's *The Life of Eleanor Marx* (Clarendon Press 1967).

Henry James's review is in *The Scenic Art*.

Joseph Hatton's report is in *Henry Irving's Impressions of America* (Sampson, Low, Marston, Searle and Remington 1884).

Edward Burne-Jones's comment is in Penelope Fitzgerald's *Edward Burne-Jones* (Michael Joseph 1975).

Nina Auerbach's analysis of the significance of the Sargent portrait is from *The Demon and the Woman* (Harvard University Press 1982).

The translation of Augustine Filon's often caustic views was published as *The English Stage* (Milne 1897).

Shaw's letter to William Archer is in Dan Laurence's edition of *Bernard Shaw: Collected Letters, Volume 2, 1898-1910* (Max Reinhardt 1972).

Bram Stoker's *Dracula* was first published by Archibald Constable in 1907. Several editions are still in print.

A. E. Wilson puts the Irving years into perspective in *The Lyceum* (Dennis Yates 1952).

ELLEN AND HENRY

Margaret Webster's comment on the relationship is from *The Same Only Different* (Gollanz 1969).

Lady Duff Gordon's reminiscence is included in *Discretions and Indiscretions* (Jarrold 1932).

CRAIG, SHAW AND A JUBILEE

Oscar Asche's description of Ellen's participation in *The Merry Wives of Windsor* is from his memoirs: *Oscar Asche* (Hurst & Blackett 1929).

Max Beerbohm's reviews are from *Around Theatres*.

W. B. Yeats's letter to Lady Gregory is in Allan Wade's edition of *The Letters of W. B. Yeats* (Rupert Hart-Davis 1954).

Basil Dean recalled the excitement of the Jubilee in *Seven Ages* (Hutchinson 1970).

L. Carson's review of *The Story of My Life* appears in *The Stage Year Book 1909*.

THE FINAL YEARS

A. E. Matthews remembered his appearance with Ellen when he wrote *Matty* (Hutchinson 1952).

W. Graham Robertson's memories come, of course. from his *Letters*.

Biographical Notes

The following brief notes are included to give some idea of the lives of some of Ellen's relations, friends and colleagues. Details are also given of some of the artists, photographers, stage and costume designers and writers whose work has been represented in this book.

FAMILY

Ben Terry (1818-96)
Ellen's father. He married Sarah Ballard (1817-1892) in 1838. They had eleven children in all, two of whom died in infancy.

Benjamin Terry (1839-?)
Ellen's brother. He possessed all the Terry charm but did not go on the stage. Instead he spent an optimistically full life drifting in and out of a succession of jobs in France, Australia and India, where he died (date unknown).

Kate Terry (1844-1924)
Ellen's eldest sister. She was on the point of becoming the leading actress of the day when she gave up working on the stage to marry Arthur Lewis, a wealthy linen-draper. Their home — Moray Lodge on Campden Hill — became a favoured meeting place for London artistic society. Kate and Arthur had four children — all girls. The eldest (also named Kate), who became the mother of Val and John Gielgud, published her autobiography *Kate Terry Gielgud* (Max Reinhardt) in 1953.

George Terry (1850-1928)
Ellen's brother. He served an apprenticeship as a cabinet-maker with Maples, the famous London 'Art Furniture' store, then joined the Lyceum Company as Master Carpenter in 1882. He later became involved in theatrical management, assisting in his brother Fred's affairs.

Miss Marion Terry.

Fred Terry as 'The Scarlet Pimpernel'.

Marion Terry (1853-1930)

Ellen's younger sister. She made her stage debut in 1873 and was an actress all her life until arthritis curtailed her career in 1923. She never married.

Florence Terry (1855-96)

Ellen's younger sister. As a child actress she understudied her sister Marion before joining the Lyceum Company to play Nerissa to Ellen's Portia in *The Merchant of Venice*. She took over Ellen's roles in *Olivia* and *New Men and Old Acres* when the Company went on tour. She retired from the stage on her marriage to a lawyer, William Morris, in 1882.

Charles Terry (1857-1933)

Ellen's younger brother. He made a successful career in theatrical management. His daughter Minnie (1882-1964) was an actress. She married Edmund Gwenn who became a Hollywood film star in middle age.

Tom Terry (1860-?)

Ellen's younger brother. He was the only member of the family to have nothing whatever to do with the stage, believing it to be 'an abomination of the devil'. He went

to sea and settled finally in Mandalay, where he became a factory manager.

Fred Terry (1864-1932)

Ellen's youngest brother. He was a handsome, charming romantic actor who first came to prominence when he played Sebastian to Ellen's Viola in *Twelfth Night* at the Lyceum. He was perfectly cast in his greatest success — *The Scarlet Pimpernel*. He married Julia Neilson (1868-1957) and both of their children, Dennis Neilson-Terry (1895-1932) and Phyllis Neilson-Terry (1892-1977) became actors.

HUSBANDS (AND LOVER)

George Frederick Watts (1817-1904)

Ellen's first husband. Watts was a leading Victorian painter, sculptor and draughtsman. His moral pieces, such as the painting 'Hope' (now in the Tate Gallery, London) and the huge statue 'Physical Energy' (in Kensington Gardens) were considered by the artist